PRECIOUS FEW CLUES

THE TRUE CRIME INVESTIGATION OF KANSAS CITY'S "PRECIOUS DOE" MURDER

MARLA BERNARD

AUTHOR OF "BY THE SIDE OF THE ROAD"

WildBluePress.com

PRECIOUS FEW CLUES published by:

WILDBLUE PRESS
P.O. Box 102440
Denver, Colorado 80250

Publisher Disclaimer: Any opinions, statements of fact or fiction, descriptions, dialogue, and citations found in this book were provided by the author, and are solely those of the author. The publisher makes no claim as to their veracity or accuracy and assumes no liability for the content.

ISBN 978-1-957288-93-2 Hardcover
ISBN 978-1-957288-94-9 Trade Paperback
ISBN 978-1-957288-92-5 eBook

Cover Design by Tatiana Vila, www.viladesign.net
Interior Formatting by Elijah Toten, www.totencreative.com

PRECIOUS FEW CLUES

The facts of the cases are taken directly from the related court documents and case files, including interviews with all parties. Some names and identifying details have been changed to protect the privacy of others. While a somewhat lengthy section of this book is allocated to actual letters written by the two killers, it is essential to provide the reader with potential insight into the personalities of individuals capable of the most insidious behaviors.

Precious Few Clues

"She broke the bread into fragments and gave them to the children, who ate with avidity. 'She hath kept none for herself,' grumbled the Sergeant. 'Because she is not hungry,' said a soldier. 'Because she is a mother,' said the Sergeant."
—Victor Hugo

I've been asked many times why I'd want to write a book about the untimely deaths of children and the grisly events that surrounded them. I've often pondered that same question, sometimes wondering what was wrong with me. Why would anyone want to tell these stories? I believe it's partially because I love to write. And partly because I had been a police officer who married a sergeant in homicide, so it's something I live with every day. Mostly, however, I believe it's because I am first and foremost focused on family and motherhood, hell-bent on keeping my family together, whatever the cost. The world never looks as terrifying or as enormous as it seems to a mother whose child is in danger. Anyone blessed to be a parent knows exactly what I mean. I can say this with certainty and conviction, as both my children were each, at separate times, lost to me for little more than one instant. Each time it was a breath-holding, heart-stopping, gut-wrenching instant that felt like it took a lifetime. These hellish experiences drove home the feeling of that instinctive mother bear protectiveness that comes from your soul's depths.

The first was when my daughter Amanda, at age three, had a febrile seizure due to what we had initially thought was merely her bad tonsils acting up again. She had been to the doctor late in the afternoon, so she stayed at grandma's house that day instead of attending preschool. A holiday of sorts for Amanda and one day's pay for me wouldn't be lost due to a sick child out of school. Amanda was happy enough about it. Have Amoxicillin, will travel. Being sick at grandma's was better than any good day at pre-school, with a semi-retired grandfather to fluff pillows and a doting grandmother to cut peanut butter sandwiches into four perfect triangles, just the way Amanda liked them. At one moment, she was seated on a pink bed sheet draped on the living room floor, happily picnicking in front of *Sesame Street* on the "electronic babysitter." The next moment, she fell backward, eyes rolling back, and breathing stopped.

A panicked phone call received at work from my brother sent words spinning around me that Amanda was being transported by ambulance to the hospital next door to where I worked. My nineteen-year-old brother happened to be at home due to a broken hand he'd sustained while working at the city jail. (Police department score that day: Jailed dirtbag one point, brother - zip). "Uncle Mikey" had tried unsuccessfully to perform one-handed resuscitation on my non-responsive child. My father didn't know CPR but had enough wits about him to realize that an electrical worker he'd seen working at the front of the home might know it, so he ran to the door and summoned the lineman. CPR was administered to Amanda by a Kansas City Power & Light worker who, by an act of fate, had just been certified in life support techniques that week. Talk about "angels unawares." Even for the inconsistently faithful Catholic like me, you have to believe in a higher power when the unexplainable occurs, the stars align, and the right people in the right place at the right time appear in your life.

While all this was transpiring, I had called my sister, who worked at that same hospital, and she met me just minutes later in the Emergency Room driveway. The ambulance ride from grandma's house to the hospital shouldn't have taken more than five minutes. Five became ten, ten rolled to twenty, but still no ambulance. With my police experience, I knew that an ambulance goes lights and sirens in a hurry but travels at normal speed if the victim is dead or in stable condition. I looked to the negative. Being raised Roman Catholic by a Sicilian father, abused as a child by an "uncle by marriage," and schooled by the Sisters of Cruel and Unusual Punishment, I was raised on guilt. It was part of my DNA—I couldn't possibly look to the bright side. Of course, losing Amanda was all I could imagine. Surely it was my fault—a penance for accidentally eating a hotdog on Friday or missing the holy water on the way out of the church before the Vatican spun the altars around and absolved us from wearing chapel caps and wool uniforms. Whatever the cause, my chest ached, and I couldn't breathe—or maybe I was holding my breath—as I stood in that driveway, not knowing what I'd find when the long-delayed ambulance finally arrived. It did arrive, and so did my beautiful Amanda.

Amanda recovered after two days in the hospital, accompanied by her mother, who slept with her hand firmly in the middle of her child's chest in a feeble attempt to monitor her breathing. (The doctor didn't think she needed a monitor, but what do they know?) She's now a mother in her own right and an excellent one. Little Michael Anthony and Isabella Rose now hold her heart in a death grip, and she often reminds me that she finally understands real love.

Several years later, my other three-year-old was "lost" in Nevada on a separate occasion. We were on a family vacation out west to visit David's beloved Aunt Mildred and Uncle Russ. They were lovely folks, the sort of family you'd love to call your own. Unfortunately for us, they lived all too many miles away. Mildred doted on David, and she'd have dealt him fits if she'd have known what transpired in good ol' Virginia City. Fortunately, it occurred after we visited Las Vegas, so what happened in Virginia City stayed in Virginia City. Aunt Mildred was none the wiser, and David retained his esteemed place as the favorite nephew.

Matthew Harrison Bernard was to go into the jail museum with his father (David's version of a busman's holiday) while Amanda and I took in an antique shop located just two storefronts down. My conversation with David went like this: "You have Matthew, right?"

"Yes."

"Hold his hand, okay?"

"Yes."

"I'm just going down here."

"Okay."

BIG SIGH – "Yes."

"Amanda's with me."

"Yes."

"I'll meet you back out here."

No response. He'd either had enough, tuned me out, or both.

After picking up a couple of *Bonanza*-esque souvenirs, Amanda and I headed back to find David. He was peering through the video camera lens, capturing images of the Old West and mannequins representing long-dead cowboys and other assorted motley characters. I asked him where Matthew was, and he said, "He's right here," and turned to look at an old wooden barrel upon which sat an empty saddle. We all began calling his name with no response. I sent Amanda back through the jail to try and locate him while I ran outside and looked for him. What was he wearing? I'd dressed him, and we hadn't packed that much. Was it a red shirt with blue stripes? I couldn't be sure. Looking out onto the great expanse of the Nevada mountainside, the world never seemed so large or frightening to me. The grandeur of the landscape that is western Nevada terrified me as I stood there. It was only seconds, but I still remember it as though it were now. I spent a decade in those moments—where was he?

Matthew managed to elude his sister in the jail museum, but he materialized on the spot when his father went back to find him. Where had WE been? Matthew was indignant. Such is the perspective of childhood. All was well in the end but rest assured that I had never told this story that I hadn't referred to it as when Matthew was "lost in the desert"!!! I found a photo of Matthew not too long ago and he was wearing the same shirt. He was holding a catch of prized sun perch and beaming with pride. The trip to Nevada. It made me cry.

My children have since grown and have become honorable young adults. Parenting is something I got better at over the years. Ta-da! If I didn't get anything else right, I nailed this one! To paraphrase the late Jacqueline Kennedy Onassis, what else matters if you mess up raising your children?

The Little Innocents

Victor Hugo said that no one ever kept a secret so well as a child. When detectives are faced with investigating the murder of a tiny, innocent victim of a violent crime, it is challenging to get clues and information. While any reasonable and prudent individual is incensed by these crimes, which are so brutal and unthinkable, more often than not, the suspects are parents, relatives, or someone close to the child. There is no cooperation from the suspect, and in many cases, family members even work to protect them, as in the "Precious Doe" case, so it is incumbent upon the detectives to develop a relationship of sorts with the child victim and gradually piece together the answers to the secret that was literally taken to the grave.

This book opens with a quote from Victor Hugo, and two others have significant meaning to this case and the countless other child murders that tragically occur yearly. First, Hugo said, "The little people must be sacred to the big ones," and "it is from the rights of the weak that the duty of the strong is comprised." Law enforcement officers are sworn to uphold the law, and nowhere is that duty more closely felt than bringing justice for child victims and being the voice for the little children who were rendered silent.

Hugo also said, "It is by suffering that human beings become angels." So at least we can gain comfort from knowing that these small victims who suffered so much are in heaven and on our side.

DESTINY'S CHILD

At the moment of commitment, the universe conspires to assist you.
—Goethe

When Sgt. David Bernard was a little kid, about three years old, he wouldn't go outside to play unless his mother helped him put on his cap gun, belt, and holsters. I don't know if it was a classic Nichols cap gun set, a Hop-A-Long Cassidy, a Roy Rogers, or a Cisco Kid's, but it was a 1950s vintage, and so was David. Even as a child, he didn't walk down "Fremont Street"without the big irons strapped to his hip. David Bernard was a born lawman. David wasn't even in kindergarten yet, but he'd stroll down the long gravel driveway of his south Kansas City home and prepare to stand up for all the little neighborhood girls who needed his protection. Ruth Bernard would never have dreamed that her little boy—sporting plastic firearms and red felt Stetson—might someday spend over half of his professional life investigating the untimely deaths of little lost girls he felt compelled to protect.

Case # 01-040862

April 28, 2001 was an unseasonably warm day in Kansas City. That's the one thing you can count on in this region. The weather can swing from warm and sunny to bitterly cold in an instant. Not unlike public sentiment. Public sentiment is with you when the winds are calm. But they can drop into single digits with no predictability and cut through you to the depths of your soul. It can't be forecast, but it's inevitable.

It was a routine "murder squad" weekend when Sgt. David Bernard and the 1020 Homicide Squad responded to the intersection of 59th Street and Kensington regarding an unknown black female found deceased in the woods. It was around 7:30 in the evening and the weather was warm and dry. It turned out that an officer had discovered a naked, decapitated child. Sgt. Bernard knew that decapitated children were rare in this country, having worked with the behavioral sciences unit of the FBI in Quantico, Virginia, on previous serial murder cases. But, being so gruesomely unusual, he knew it would be a media firestorm. So four of the 1020 detectives were called in, and one from Overland Park, Kansas, who was shadowing the squad at the time. This case was baptism by fire for that poor guy if there ever was such a thing!

When they arrived at the scene, the squad gathered at a church parking lot across from the wooded crime scene.

They were briefed by the patrol officers who had responded to the original call. There, they learned those district officers had been dispatched to a nearby address on a missing older adult who'd wandered away from home earlier that evening. Officers began checking eight acres of dense brush. The vacant land, situated in the middle of the inner-city, had become a makeshift trash dump with a dirt and gravel road in the center used by water department employees to access drainage lines, making it very convenient for illegal dumpers. When officers checked down that road, it was dusk, but the older man was nowhere in sight. Police Officer Jason Rusley spotted what appeared to be a doll lying off to the side of the road in an area covered with dense weeds. He approached it and saw a child's body lying on its stomach, naked and with its head gone. Fly eggs were already deposited on the gaping neck wound that exposed the child's spine. At 4:54 pm, the high was 81 degrees, and the temperature was 69 by midnight. It wasn't surprising to detectives that flies were gathering in the warmth and that larvae and maggots had begun to hatch.

The obvious questions were asked. Where's the head? Where's the clothing? Was a piece of a dress or panties hanging up on something nearby? They couldn't find anything. Why put the body here instead of walking six paces further into the brush where the body might never have been found? It was as though this child was a piece of trash, no different than any of the old tires nearby, only to be discarded when no longer of use. Officers cordoned off the crime scene and called the Homicide Unit. The 1020 Homicide squad was up to bat.

Bernard, a seasoned violent crimes sergeant, kicked into action, assuming his usual "all business" mode. The situation was so surreal the horror of it didn't hit him yet as he systematically started the wheels in motion to initiate the processing of the crime scene. He showed no emotion when he began methodically detailing the steps to take and handing out assignments. It would be a long time before the steely mask he wore would crack and show the impact on him—body and soul.

Broken Doll

It was a grisly scene. In a clearing, the little girl's body was lying naked, face down. The head had been severed at the base of her neck and her spinal cord was visible in the jagged, rough cut made by some unknown object. Her head wasn't anywhere in the immediate area. There was only a little blood on the victim's back, legs, and arms, and no large pools or blood trails could be seen. Her entire back and legs had bruises and discolorations. Looping scars on her back and torso were most likely caused by a clothes hanger or cord. Someone had severely beaten this child. She had already started to decompose in the warm, damp woods. There were maggots and larvae in the neck wound and around her vagina, anus, and armpits—they sought out anywhere warm and moist.

The following is the narrative of the initial homicide investigative report taken by Detective Wayne Jones relative to the dead body of an unknown black female child discovered in the woods. Note that all grammatical and spelling errors are from the original documents, not the author's errors.

"On 04-28-2001 at about 2000 hours Sgt. D. Bernard, Det. M. Hutcheson, Det. R. Rickett, Det. K. Kirchhoff, and the reporting Detective responded to 59 th and Kensington on the above captioned case.

Upon arrival contact was made with P.O. Rusley radio # 213, and P.O. Dennis radio # 213(A). P.O. Rusley stated on 04-28-2001 at 1842 hours he and P.O. Dennis were dispatched as a two person car to 4301 E. 59th street to check the welfare of an elderly male who had been reported to have wandered off northbound into the woods at 59 th and Kensington. P.O. Rusley stated that he and P.O. Dennis observed a car path at 59th and Kensington leading northbound into the wooded area. P.O. Rusley stated that the car path was secured by a large cable making it inaccessible to vehicle traffic. P.O. Rusley stated that they then walked the car path approximately 100 yards and were advised that the elderly male had been located at 59th and Elmwood. P.O. Rusley stated that he and P.O. Dennis then turned around and began walking southbound on the car path towards 59th street. P.O. Rusley stated that he then observed the victim lying face down, naked in a clearing, approximately seven feet to the west of the car path with no signs of life. P.O. Rusley stated that the victim's head had been severed and did not observe the victim's head anywhere close to the body.

There was a large heavy dense wooded area observed on the north side of 59th Street. There was a dirt and gravel car path that was observed at 59 th street and Kensington. The car path was secured by a large cable that was cut by Crime Scene Investigators to allow access for their equipment. The wooded area extended an undetermined range to the east and west of the car path. The car path extended from 59 th Street to the north, into a clearing, where the car path ended. The wooded area extended to the north of the clearing an indeterminate range. The car path was approximately 350 feet long. There were large tire tracks observed on the car path that extended from 59 th Street into the clearing. The tire tracks appeared to be caused by large maintenance type vehicles. None of the tire tracks appeared new.

There were numerous trash items observed in the wooded area to both the east and west of the car path, and along the car path. There were also numerous torn or cut clothing items, along with trash observed in the clearing, where the car path ended. There were two dark colored rags/ possible clothing items at the northwest end of the clearing. There was a dark colored piece of material/ possible children clothing at the far north end of the clearing. There was a pair of an unknown child's green cotton sweatpants at the northeast end of the clearing.

The victim was observed to be approximately 175 feet to the north of 59th street, in the wooded area, out seven feet to the west of the car path. The victim appeared to be a female child about five years of age. The victim was lying naked, face down, in a clearing. The victim's head had been severed and was not observed within the vicinity of the victim's body. The victim's upper torso was facing toward the northwest and the victim's feet were facing toward the southeast. The victim's left arm was underneath her body and her left hand was resting near her left thigh and crotch. There was an apparent faded skin line formed at the waistline on the victim where she would most likely be wearing her panties. There was apparent minute blood drops observed about the victim's back, legs and arms. There was apparent bruising and discoloration on the victim's upper back. There was apparent discoloration observed to the victim's lower back, bottom, and the upper back of her legs. There was an apparent looping scar observed on the left side of the victim's torso. There were also apparent looping scars observed on the victim's back. It appeared the looping scars were possibly caused by a clothes hanger or cord. The victim's body appeared to be in early stages of decomposition. There was larva observed about the victim's vagina anus, and armpits. There was larva and maggots forming at the area where the victim's head was severed. The victim's head was severed just above where the base of her neck connects to her torso. There was apparent blood observed at the origin of where the victim's head was severed. The upper part of *the victim's spinal cord was observed at the origin of where the head was severed. There was also what appeared to be loose skin at the neck area of where the head was severed. There was no indication of apparent blood on the ground beneath where the victim's head had been severed. The origin of where the victim's head was severed appeared to be jagged and not caused by a smooth cutting tool. There were no signs of apparent blood observed within the immediate vicinity of the victim's body.*

OST Lutman and CST VanRyan responded and processed the scene. The Missouri Search and Rescue it responded with K-9's and canvassed the area for any evidence with negative results. The Missouri Search and Rescue Unit again responded to the location on 04-29-2001 at 0700 hours to again canvass the area during daylight hours with negative results.

Investigator Chris Watkins, of the Jackson County Medical Examiner's Office, responded to process the scene. Kansas City Motorcycle Escort responded to transport the victim to the Medical Examiner's Office."

At this point, Sgt. Bernard decided to withhold critical information from the media regarding the fact that the child had been decapitated. As he later described it in his testimony at the killer's trial, his reasoning made perfect sense. Such a confounding situation necessitated thoughtful planning.

"Well, I knew that the media really hadn't focused on this yet, especially I knew once it got out that the little girl was decapitated, that it was really going to be something the media was going to put out and cover a lot in depth. I knew from past experience that when you get a highly publicized case, from working highly publicized cases in the past and working on task forces, that once it's out there, the public will start hopefully giving you information, but generally it

comes in such a number, an immense amount of telephone calls and letters, that you're just going to be overwhelmed with all this information unless you do something quickly to get a handle on it."

There was a large group of people standing around the crime scene. A woman in the crowd of onlookers said she watched two kids, a 10-year-old girl and an 8-year-old boy, for a friend who lived in one of the houses on Kensington. She stated she'd been at the house since 8:00 a.m. the day before and spent the night there. On this particular day, she had gotten up at around 10:00 a.m. and confirmed that the children were at the residence and in good condition. In addition, she indicated that she had no information about missing people in the area. An officer at the scene verified the woman's statement, making a visual identification for his report.

Five men gathered nearby, and all but one said they lived in the neighborhood and didn't know anything about anyone missing. No one had any information. One refused to give his address. "Didn't know nothin'. Ain't did nothin'." The typical singsong at most crime scenes. Another guy refused to say anything and just walked away. During the attempt to gather information from the bystanders, detectives were approached by an unknown black male wearing a Time Warner Cable work shirt. He told them they had no right to talk to these people or the children gathering outside the crime scene. Then he told all the kids not to speak to the police and leave the area before anyone tried to talk to them. Several kids left the area as others refused to speak to the police. The man later got into a pick-up truck and drove off. Not involving community members to help solve a crime against one of their own seemed unjust, especially for an innocent child abandoned in the woods. Was there no one willing to help?

Into the Woods

As the person in charge, one of Bernard's first actions was to call in the Crime Scene Unit. Detectives arrived and roped off the area. As the sun went down, a trailer with a generator and spotlights was brought in to help illuminate the already dark and ominous woods that concealed who-knows-what in the shadows. It was like the wall of thorns and vines that hid Sleeping Beauty, but this gruesome thicket was not a fairytale. Instead, it was the stuff of nightmares and this sleeping princess would never awaken from her forced slumber. The body was located about 170 to 180 feet north of 59th Street and about eight feet west of the gravel road into the woods. There was no visible blood and the body was not stiff with rigor mortis. The area was sprayed with luminol, a water-based chemical routinely used by forensic investigators to detect trace amounts of blood at crime scenes, causing the blood to fluoresce a pale blue color, but no trail of blood was found. Disappointingly, there wasn't even any blood near the body, indicating that it was simply a disposal site and nothing more.

It was then that Bernard called in a team of specialized canine handlers. Using human remains detection dogs in that environment would be one of the quickest and best approaches to locating any evidence, most significantly the child's decapitated head. The Missouri Search and Rescue group, an all-volunteer, non-profit dog/handler unit, responded to the scene. These canine teams hold certifications that meet or exceed the Scientific Working Group on Dog and Orthogonal Detector Guidelines (SWGDOG) recommended guidelines, so their assistance is invaluable to investigators. It was dense, rugged terrain to navigate, especially in the dark of night, but the teams searched anyway. The handlers tied luminous chemical sticks to the dogs' collars to keep them in sight, and together they searched the stifling, thick woods ripe with garbage and decay. The K9 handlers said it was the roughest brush they had ever searched. Human scents are, in a way, like liquids in that they "flow" to low-lying areas and "pool" into a vapor that lingers. Cadaver dogs are sent to the most likely places where this would occur, tracking the scent both on the ground and in the air. Because of their specialized training, cadaver dogs can identify crime scenes even if the body has since been moved; unfortunately, this time, the area would prove to be only a repository for the child's remains and not the scene of the crime. Because the initial search didn't reveal anything, the group disbanded with the plan to recheck the area in daylight.

At midnight, the search was called off because the darkness worked against them. The plan was that the search teams would all re-group at the church at 7:00 a.m. It would not be the usual Sunday gathering one comes to expect in a church parking lot. There would be no affirmations from the "Amen pew" in this investigation for four long years. Yet, despite the late hour, officers could hear children laughing and playing in the distance. Was there a connection between this tiny victim and those whose voices echoed in the night?

Because this was not an easily accessible or well-known area, Sgt. Bernard thought the child was most likely local and that a missing child would be reported sooner or later. Someone would call the police in search of a little girl lost. Who wouldn't report a missing child? She was young, and statistics show that the younger the victim, the closer the killer is to the family—a parent, boyfriend, or immediate family member. Young children are usually protected, and stranger killings are uncommon. Best guess, given the level of brutality, one could assume either the child's father or the mother's boyfriend was the suspect. A female rarely resorts to that level of mutilation, especially a child. Surely someone, somewhere, knew something and would come forward. As soon as the child was identified and detectives determined who had care and control of her at the time of death, the case would quickly be solved, or so it was thought. Time proved it wrong.

More Than Junk in The Trunk

It was a bumper crop of homicides for the murder squad that week in April. It was only the 117th day of the year, and the city had already experienced its 28th homicide. First, a female body was found in the trunk of her boyfriend's car on Friday night, April 27th, the night before the decapitated child was found. She had already begun to liquefy, but the stench was chalked up to what he claimed was a horrible natural gas leak in the neighborhood. It begged the question, "Which part of the landfill did he live in?" The victim's remains were already a decomposition soup when the suspect drove her mother around in the car to "help look for her." What the investigation uncovered was challenging to comprehend and would ultimately complicate the early days of the Precious Doe case.

During the late afternoon of Friday, April 27, 2001, police received an anonymous phone call in which the caller stated that he wanted to give information about a body in the trunk of a brown 1984 four-door Mercedes Benz automobile. The caller said the car was propped up on bricks at a house near 58th Street and College Avenue. The informant said he was casing that neighborhood to steal the wheels of a Mercedes that appeared to be abandoned when he noticed the trunk was ajar. When he opened it, he saw what seemed to be a decaying body. He insisted that he may have been a thief, but he was not a murderer and felt police needed to be aware of the situation. Patrol officers were sent to check the vicinity for anything that possibly matched the caller's claims.

Officers canvassing the area successfully located a Mercedes on cinder blocks in a fenced-in yard at 56XX College Avenue. The house had burned in 2000 and was boarded up and posted by authorities as a dangerous building. The officers noticed a foul odor at the site and investigated the yard. Unfortunately, they discovered the decomposed body when they opened the vehicle's trunk.

Police determined that the abandoned house and the vehicle containing the body belonged to Reginald P. Morrow, an unemployed 34-year-old Black male with a criminal record. When officers contacted neighbors, they were told that people in the area suspected Morrow of being a child molester and arrest records confirmed that he had a previous arrest for a sex offense. The suspect had been staying with a female friend and her three daughters at 5XXX E. 28th St. One daughter, Shanda Renae Wilson, an 18-year-old Black female, had been missing since March 2, 2001. It appeared that the body in the trunk was most likely related to the disappearance of Shanda Wilson. Still, dental records were required to make an identification due to the condition of the human remains.

As witnesses were interviewed, they all confirmed that the suspect had been driving the Mercedes recently, and they had noticed a foul odor which he explained away as a natural gas leak in the area where he parked the vehicle. He even went so far as to take the victim's mother on errands in the car, using the same explanation for the horrific smell.

When word got out that police were looking for Morrow, he ultimately fled to Pine Bluff, Arkansas where his daughter lived. It was determined that he was traveling in a rental car and was accompanied by a female passenger. The KCPD sent this information to Arkansas authorities and a manhunt was soon underway. Unfortunately, in another ironic twist of bad timing, people would manage to mistakenly associate this case with the child's decapitated body in the woods up in Kansas City. These, however, were two separate and distinct crimes and the 1020 squad knew it.

Around 9:00 a.m. on April 29th, the day after Precious Doe's body was found, the Pine Bluff, Arkansas police located the rental vehicle outside a motel where it was placed under surveillance. After a few hours, an individual fitting Morrow's description exited the motel and attempted to get into the rental vehicle. When police tried to approach him, he fled on foot before stopping, drawing a revolver, and shooting himself in the right temple. Morrow died of a self-inflicted gunshot wound rather than being taken into police custody. Upon checking the motel room where he was staying, police discovered a 16-year-old female from Kansas City who indicated that she and Morrow had been romantically involved for over a year. When officers determined that she was a runaway from Kansas City, she was taken into protective custody until family members could travel from Missouri to Arkansas and take charge of her.

Morrow had a large, rusty fishing knife among his belongings. Without consulting the KCPD, Pine Bluff officers somehow determined the weapon was involved in the beheading of the unnamed girl in Kansas City and released this theory to the press. The only connection was that both crimes had occurred in Kansas City. One didn't have anything to do with the other case, but the Pine Bluff police announced that they had solved the Kansas City child murder, notwithstanding.

The knife was recovered and sent to the KCPD Crime Lab for testing. The following is taken from the report on the findings. Note that all grammatical and spelling errors are from the original documents, not the author's errors.

"KNIFE AND CASE

This item was a knife and sheath received from the Pine Bluff, Arkansas, Police Department. This item was shipped via Federal Express on tracking number 826400336322. This item was collected under Pine Bluff PD case number 01—327.

The knife was of a style that had a compass on the butt end. The compass part would unscrew, allowing access to a compartment in the handle. Within this compartment was a plastic bag containing fishing line and hooks. This compartment appeared to have had minimal access due to paint flaking from the threads, and the plastic bag appeared to be in the original folded arrangement. A blue polyester fiber and a natural fiber were collected from inside this compartment.

The blade of the knife had a large blade that curved to a pointed tip with serrations opposite the cutting bevel. Material had accumulated in the serrations, suggesting no recent attempts to clean the knife. No blood was observed within this material in the serrations. Soil was present on the face of the blade near the tip.

No hair was observed on any part of this knife. No blood was detected using a presumptive test over areas of the blade and handle.

The sheath was leather with a compartment for a honing stone. A honing stone was present in this compartment. No bloodstains were observed on this sheath."

Despite evidence to the contrary, the media assumed that the dead girl must have been the child's mother. This curveball wasn't even close enough to the target to win a cigar for consolation, but the story made for excellent copy.

Sgt. Bernard was forced to deal with the press, insisting that there was no way the two cases were linked. He tried to get them to look at the sophistication of the crimes. The killer drove around with his dead girlfriend in the car until she liquefied. If he did something that stupid, he obviously wasn't smart enough to take steps to undress the child and dump her body in one spot and the head in another. Here was the headless body of a child in a wooded area on Saturday night. Someone would be missing a little girl. Or would they?

In the wee hours of Sunday morning, Sgt. Bernard had just sat down in his recliner to eat something, rest, and take up the Kensington Street case when the sun came back up. Then one call after another came into his cell phone—the start of hundreds of calls over the following hours, days, and months. The ringtone became the clarion call to horror. Put your life on hold and follow the Sirens' song, beckoning you into the depths of someone's personal Hell. Such was the world he lived in, and only God and a suspect knew what awaited the murder squad on every new call. There did not seem to be sufficient numbers of coins for the Ferryman of Death, but detectives paid an enormous price for the ride, notwithstanding. The proverbial pound of flesh would be spent, but detectives would somehow manage to retain custody of their souls despite it all.

Two murders didn't seem enough to satisfy the demons of death. The 1020 squad would pick up a new case involving a guy in a car trunk by Sunday afternoon. Detectives were sent to the city's west side to work on that case. A Kansas City, Kansas gang member had been shot and thrown into the trunk of a car. No leads. What else was new? Car trunks appeared to be the storage method of choice that month. See the USA in your Chevrolet. Store a cadaver in your Cavalier.

Who Are You?

While part of the squad pursued the new case of another body in another car, the area canvasses began in earnest in the area of 59th and Kensington. By the time the case was over, the 1020 squad would have conducted the most extensive area canvass in the department's history. Unfortunately, knocking on all those doors resulted in little more than spent shoe leather and exhausted detectives. The reports all read the same. "No answer. Left a business card." "No answer. Left a business card." "...did not see or hear anything suspicious in the neighborhood the past few days." "Had not heard of any missing children in the area." "...didn't have any information." "Vacant lot." "House appeared vacant." "Refused to give name or information." "No information." "No information." "Heard the dogs bark...maybe someone was in the woods but wasn't sure." "Saw city trucks going into and out of the woods where the victim was found during the week."

A few years later, it would be determined that one specific door they knocked on during the May 8, 2001 area canvass would be particularly interesting. The file notation from the contact that detectives made with the residents read, "Michelle Johnson, 816-XXX-2XXX, Rachelle Allendale." They claimed to have seen "a Black male wearing a red/white/green striped shirt and cut-off blue jeans with short hair, 20-25 years old, walking in the area at appx. 0800 hours on 04/27/01." They might as well have claimed he was with Elvis Presley and Bigfoot, for the truth could not have been farther from their story.

It wasn't long before the local news outlets found out about the headless little girl, and it was a media-feeding frenzy. The story was everywhere. The prior week's case of a female victim in the car was beckoning on Monday morning. They had good leads on this, and it had to be worked, which demanded the squad's attention most of that day. The spare time—as though they had any—was split between dodging the news crews and planning the continued search for the decapitated little girl's identity and the gruesome work of finding her head. Some freaky child killers might have kept it as a souvenir for all they knew. It's a bizarre and common trait that all serial killers seem to possess and there was the remote possibility that this might not be an isolated incident. Only God knew if the woods on Kensington Avenue hid more victims, and God seemed to be preoccupied that weekend while Satan danced in Kansas City—the Heart of America.

The Body - Part One

After the child's body was transported to the medical examiner's office, the KCPD Crime Lab staff undertook the gruesome tasks of recovering evidence and photographing the body.

The report taken at that time noted that *"...the body had numerous bruises, semi-circular and linear type marks on her torso, back, arms, legs, and feet. An area of apparent bruising covered her lower back, buttocks, and upper thighs. Insect larvae were located at the opening of her vagina, between her buttocks, and in the gaping wound above her neckline."*

It stated, *"Swabs were collected as items #1 and 2 from both inner thighs. Apparent blood spatter was observed on the victim's upper back and on the backside of her right shoulder. A swab was collected as item #3 from this blood spatter."* After recovering the items they'd collected, the body was released to an investigator with the Jackson County Medical Examiner's office.

The discarded body was at least now documented for the record as something more than somebody's trash that had been lying naked and covered with maggots. This child would soon be named Precious Doe and she now had a safe place to lie, even under a white sheet on a cold gurney. She was treated with dignity, something she'd been denied at the end of her brief time on this earth. She died the death of an old rag doll.

The day following the victim's discovery, Det. Wayne Jones responded to the medical examiner's office for the first autopsy, that of the headless torso of the unnamed little girl. Dr. Thomas Young was the Jackson County Medical Examiner at the time and he performed the first medical examination. The following is an excerpt from Jones's written account of the examination of the body: Note that all grammatical and spelling errors are from the original documents, not the author's errors.

"The victim's body was observed to be naked lying face down on a white shroud atop of a stainless steel exam table. There were some branches and leaves observed lying on the white shroud next to the victim. There was maggot activity at the origin of where the victim's head was severed. The victim's head was severed at the upper middle portion of the victim's neck. There was apparent larva in both of the victim's armpits. There was apparent larva also observed on the victim's left hand. The victim was wearing a yellow identification bracelet on her left forearm.

There was what appeared to be bruising discoloration, and apparent abrasions about the upper back of the victim. There were apparent looping scars observed about the victim's lower back and upper rear legs. There were also apparent old scars and apparent abrasions observed to the buttocks of the victim. There were apparent old scars on the back of the victim's legs. There were apparent circular scars on the victim's right calf. There was apparent darkened discoloration observed to the victim's lower back, buttocks and the upper rear thighs. There was apparent scar in the shape of a rectangle observed to the lower right side of the victim's back above the right hip. There was apparent blood drops observed about the backside of the victim's back.

There were numerous abrasions observed about the victim's left arm. There was an apparent abrasion observed on the victim's right elbow. There also appeared to be bruising to the victim's right arm. There were also some apparent abrasions observed to the victim's right hand. There was an apparent abrasion observed on the victim's right index finger.

There was some apparent larva about the crotch and vagina area of the victim. There was an apparent laceration observed to the victim's vagina. There was some unknown fluid observed in the victim's vagina. There was also apparent scars observed on both inner thighs of the victim's legs.

There were apparent abrasions observed on the top of both of the victim's feet. There was an abrasion observed on the top of the victim's right foot that was surrounded by a yellowish discoloration on the skin.

There was an apparent laceration observed at the front base of the neck area near the origin of where the head was severed.

There was an apparent birthmark of a half-moon observed on the front left shoulder of the victim."

The medical examiner, a forensic pathologist, had thoroughly examined the child, who was African American and appeared to be between 3 and 6 years old. There were no signs of trauma to her internal organs that would have resulted in her death. He concluded that her head was severed after she died, so the decapitation didn't kill her either. He determined this based on the lack of bleeding around the main blood vessels in the neck area. His examination also revealed vertebral damage consistent with a cutting tool. Multiple superficial lacerations were evident, indicating unsuccessful attempts at cutting the child's neck. Whoever had decapitated this child worked hard at the task at hand. The head was severed from the back to the front of the neck.

It seemed that the killer's cowardice was such that they didn't want to look the child in the face. In old wives' tales, it's believed the face of a killer is imprinted on the eyes of a victim. Was the fear from folklore, or was this because the child was well known to the murderer?

The small child's body had bruises and the beginning of scars where injuries had begun to heal. It appeared that she had been beaten repeatedly, and the looping injuries were in different stages of healing. Once the whole story was uncovered, the abuse would be revealed—or at least most of it. The autopsy revealed yet another level of abuse that was not immediately visible. The following is an excerpt from that report.

"A gaping laceration extends along the posterior wall of the vagina adjacent to the posterior fourchette. This will be described in greater detail below………… Most of the posterior wall of the vagina is intact: however, a lacerated pouch is formed posterior to the posterior wall of the vagina. The posterior fourchette laceration described above provides the opening to this lacerated pouch. There is no penetration of the anus or rectum. This defect, upon opening, is 1-1/2 inches in circumference and 3/4 inch deep. The defect lies at the squamo-mucosal junction of the vagina and perineum. The soft tissues in this defect reveal areas of hemorrhage."

No one ever owned up to the sexual abuse that was evident. When the dots finally connected, it wasn't hard to guess who the probable perpetrator was of those crimes. The same individual who decapitated and tossed her amongst a pile of festering garbage had also sexually violated her.

Later that day, Detectives Danny Phillips and Wayne Jones met with Tom Hensley, an investigator with the Jackson County Medical Examiner's office. He assisted the detectives in photographing an unusual crescent-shaped birthmark on the child's left shoulder, described as "approximately one inch wide and three-quarters of an inch tall." It was released to the media, hoping that someone would recognize it and notify the TIPS Hotline. No one did.

Life Is a Circus

On Tuesday morning, May 1, 2001, police academy recruits were assigned to the Kensington Avenue crime scene to conduct a field search of the area. Shoulder to shoulder, they canvassed the site without any results. The local media showed up en-masse. There were people everywhere and the bustling activity projected a carnival atmosphere. There was even a guy who set up a cart and was selling funnel cakes. The stark reality of what transpired in those woods must not have set in with the casual observers. However, crime scene investigators knew far too well what grisly details had already been uncovered. Now, they set about the grim task of combing the debris and decay in the hope of finding anything that might reveal itself to be a clue to identifying the dead child.

At the same time, officers were interviewing a man named Billy Stegall, who claimed he had a vision about this case and that he would find the child's head. Stegall wasn't a foreign figure to the police. He was a strange duck who had shown up and participated in the Carita Johnson search. (Carita Johnson was another murder victim whose cold case the 1020 squad would later pick up and solve during the Precious Doe years.) Stegall told officers that a good way the killer would hide a knife would be to push the blade into the ground and step on it. Why did he say that? Was he involved? His background check indicated he was a Vietnam vet and postal worker (I swear this is true) who was in trouble for striking his supervisor. He had also been known to threaten to shoot everyone at work. He was one more eccentric character in the bizarre case that was unfolding. After all, what else could top the funnel cake huckster if not a disgruntled postal worker/psychic/body hunter?

The more the officers talked to Stegall, the stranger he got. Finally, a female reporter from one of the many news crews roaming about asked Billy what he was doing and followed him into a section of woods located east of where the body was found. Walking with a cane from old war injuries, Stegall navigated the woods reasonably well. He claimed he heard bees and saw a trash bag tossed in the center of an old tire. Stegall picked up the bag and placed it on a large rock. He used the cane to poke around at the contents and accidentally made holes in it, announcing to the reporter that he had discovered the head. This incident just seemed too weird to be coincidental.

The news crew summoned the police, who responded and backed everyone away from the area and notified the Homicide Unit. Sgt. Bernard was in a meeting with Dirk Tarpley and John Brunell from the FBI to request the bureau's help so they accompanied him to the scene on Kensington Avenue. John Wilson from the KCPD crime lab also responded. Wilson had the grim task of looking inside and photographing it—David's partner from his years in the tactical unit, Sgt. Carl Cherry of the Crime Scene Unit carried the head in the bag to the crime scene van.

Dirk Tarpley offered FBI assistance and Bernard took him up on it. Tarpley had become a good friend to Bernard over the years of working cases together. A rather macabre way of developing a social circle, but such are the lives of those whose work draws them into the abyss called "Murder." The plan would be that the KCPD would handle the local investigation, and the FBI would cover the out-of-state inquiries. A good leader knows that it's not about control or territory—it's about maximizing resources to achieve the desired result and these guys were the best in this grisly business. With his team falling into place, Sgt. Bernard began to formulate a plan.

Scene of the Crime

When Bernard and the investigators he brought with him arrived at the scene of the possible location of the victim's severed head, Police Officer Anthony told them that NBC Fox 4 News was filming something when he arrived. He was approached by a Black male named Billy Stegall, who said he had located the trash bag containing the victim's severed head and pointed Anthony toward the wooded area at 59th and Cypress. The officer saw a black trash bag that Stegall had placed on a rock. Stegall claimed he found it tucked inside an old tire. Despite the news crews, the onlookers, and Stegall tromping around, Anthony protected the possible crime scene until the homicide unit could get there. The whole area was nothing but thick woods and underbrush.

The new crime scene was two blocks southeast of where the body had been found. Investigators had to navigate an embankment to get to the path where the head was located. The woods were a mini-trash dump, filled with discarded tires and trash, old clothing, and a tiny victim tossed out like a broken baby doll. Only this time, the little doll was real. Someone had intentionally tried to hide the identity of this child. There was a 90-degree drop into a ravine just to the north. If the suspect had put forth just a bit more effort, who knows how long it would have taken to make this horrific new discovery. What they intended to do was not sophisticated or organized. The intent. It would come into play much later once the case got to trial.

The bag containing the unknown head was observed sitting on a flat rock directly in front of a tire which Stegall pointed out was where the bag had been hidden. There were actually two black trash bags containing the unknown head. The outer bag had been torn open and the inner bag had a small tear. The two bags had been tied together in one knot. The stench of death had drawn flies all over the bag and the adjacent area. Wilson and Bernard sprayed the area with luminol to try and locate the site where the decapitation occurred. The medical examiner would later document that she'd been there less than 48 hours and noted that she had an infection in her blood from an infection somewhere in her body. The little girl was sick on top of everything else. How or why she was ill was another question for the pile of unknowns that just kept mounting up. There was no blood in or around the area so this was ruled out as the original crime location. How did this little child come to this location?

At the scene, detectives talked to Stegall, who claimed that he went to the woods around 8:00 a.m. that day to search for the decapitated head because he was a self-described disabled veteran from the Army and had a gift at tracking and finding things in the woods. He believed this unusual talent would make him the perfect person to locate the child's head. Stegall spoke of how he smelled a foul odor emanating from the wooded area to the south, but he couldn't find anything when he searched through the brush, so he went to the north side to look around. Around 10:00 a.m., he noticed that Fox 4 News had a camera crew on 59th Street, and they followed him when he walked to the north side and wandered down the gravel access road used by the city's water services trucks. Stegall then said that he walked in a "zigzag" in the woods, trying to cover the area where the body had been carried. He walked toward a ravine in the wooded area, and in the clearing he noticed a large swarm of flies covering a black trash bag tossed into an old tire. Stegall approached the bag, said it had an overpowering smell, and "knew" he'd found the decapitated head. He poked at the bag with his cane and tore it slightly. Stegall then went back and got the camera crew and said that he had found the head. He took the camera crew back to the area and showed them what he had encountered before anyone contacted the police about what might have been found. Stegall quickly said that he had never picked up the bag and that there was no way anyone would find his fingerprints on it.

When the police finally took control of the new crime scene, Crime Scene Technician/Sgt. Carl Cherry and Crime Scene Technician Thompson responded and processed the scene. The Medical Examiner's Office was notified, and Investigator Chris Watkins responded to the location and took control of the shocking discovery. Kansas City Motorcycle Escort, a local mortuary transport service, responded and transported the bag containing the unidentified head to the Jackson County Medical Examiner's Office. God willing, this was the original victim's head and not another discarded body. One dead child was sickening. Multiple dead children would have been outrageous.

The following is the narrative portion of Crime Scene Technician Melissa Thompson's report on May 1, 2001, when a head was discovered during the morning search. Note that all grammatical and spelling errors are from the original documents, not the author's errors.

"On 05/01/2001 at 1230 hours I was dispatched to 59 th Street and Cypress, in regard to a homicide. While in route I noted a temperature of 85 degrees with sunny skies. Upon arrival I contacted P.O. Anthony who stated that trash bags containing a head had been located within the wooded area along the north side of 59:h Street, between Cypress Avenue to the west, and Cypress Place to the east. Information was

received that this was possibly the head that was missing from the body of a homicide victim discovered at 4301 E 59 St., on 04/28/2001. Det. Jones R-1025 responded and requested the scene be processed. Special Agent John Brunell with the FBI, and Chief Criminalist John Wilson with the Kansas City, Missouri Crime Laboratory also responded to the scene.

My investigation revealed the scene to be the located on the north side of 59 th Street, approximately 133 feet east of the east curb of Cypress Ave. The scene was a thickly wooded area with overgrown trees, shrubs, and other ground vegetation. The area also appeared to be used as a local dump with trash, debris, household items, and automotive parts scattered throughout the entire wooded area. The area to the south of 59 th Street was predominantly residential, however no houses were located directly across the street from where the victim's head was found. A wooden privacy fence was along the south side of 59 :h Street across from the scene. The fence was at the top of an incline and extended from Cypress Place, to approximately half way down the block towards Cypress Ave. Three overhead streetlights were located along the south curb of E. 59 th Street, between Cypress Ave., and Cypress Place. A fourth overhead streetlight was located along the east curb of Cypress Ave., just south of 59th Street, and a fifth overhead street light was located along the east curb Of Cypress Place, just south of 59th Street. It is unknown if the lights are functional due to our investigation being during day light hours.

I directed my attention to the wooded area along the north side of the road, approximately 45 feet north from the north curb of 59 th Street. I observed a black plastic trash bag resting on a rock. It appeared to be double bagged with knots tied at the top of the bags. The outer bag was slightly opened, and the Inner bag completely covered the head. The trash bags were somewhat transparent and an ear could be seen though the inner bag. The bag measured

42'8" north of the north curb of E. 59th Street, and 132 0 8" east of east curb of S. Cypress Ave. Information was received that the trash bag had been moved prior to my arrival. A discarded rubber automobile tire was laying on a rock approximately 4 feet directly north from trash bag. The tire was hollow without an attached wheel. The bag with the victim's head was reportedly found lying within the center of the tire. Flies and maggot infestation were present inside and around the trash bag. Investigator Curtis Boyd with the County responded to conduct his examination of the scene, The bags were left intact and the head was not removed from them prior to being transported to the morgue, per the request of the Medical Examiner, Dr. Young. The trash bag containing the head was carefully placed in a large brown paper bag and transported by the Kansas City Motorcycle Escort Service to the Jackson County morgue.

At this time myself and the other investigating detectives responded directly to the morgue. Upon arrival I observed the brown paper bag with the victim's head lying on a hospital gurney. The trash bag was removed from the bag and placed back on the gurney to be examined. The two trash bags were carefully removed as not to disturb the tied ends. The two (2) black plastic trash bags were collected as Item #1. The victim's head was observed to be that of an unknown black female child. The head was in the beginning stages of decomposition with some bloating and discoloration observed, Some maggot infestation was also observed. The victim's hair was braided only in the front, with one braid on each side of her forehead, extending down from the center of the top of her head. Head hair standards were collected as Item #1. A small piece of plastic was observed on the left side of the head, within the harr, and it was collected as Item #3. The victim's head had been severed just below the chin, at base of the head, with no neck portion being observed. The top front left tooth was chipped along its outer bottom edge.

The severed section of the neck from the victim's body that was discovered on 04/28/2001 was compared to the severed section of the head. One-half (1/2) of a single -vertebra was located at the severed point of each. The opposing sections of the severed bones were photographed.

The hair was removed in order to examine for any trauma or injuries, with the following being observed:

Shallow lacerations were observed across the base of the back of the head, just above where it was severed;

Other lacerations were observed along the right side of the head at the base near the severed area;

An approximate 3/16" laceration was on the top of the back of the head;

An approximate 3/4" circular lacerated area was on the top of the head;

An approximate W' circular lacerated wound was on the right temple;

An approximate 1/3" lacerated wound was on the top right side of the head;

A laceration was on the back of the right ear.

Photographs were taken of the scene and of the head at the morgue with the Nikon Coolpix 990 digital camera, with the memory card being forwarded to the Kansas City, Missouri Police Crime Laboratory. The collected items were placed in the locked vault within the CSIS property room."

Small plastic flowers, stuffed animals, cards, and balloons accumulated in the park as a makeshift memorial to the nameless child in the woods. Ultimately this little playground would become the site of vigils, birthday remembrances, and community marches.

The city ached for the fragile remains of a child who no one had come forth to claim. The entire *Heart of America* was now breaking over this lost girl.

Getting the Head Examined

At the morgue, the medical examiner conducted the autopsy of the head and determined that she was an African American female with tightly curled hair pulled into short braids. He ordered X-rays of the skull and determined that a portion of her third cervical vertebra had been severed, matching the injury to the body recovered in the exact location at 59th and Kensington. Therefore, he determined the head and body belonged to the same person.

At the request of the FBI, her head was examined and X-rayed by a forensic odontologist. He determined that she was between 3-6 years old. She had a complete set of baby teeth and one had a chip. Investigators would learn that, too, had apparently happened when her head was pitched in the trash. The following is the report provided to the medical examiner's office. Note that all grammatical and spelling errors are from the original documents, not the author's errors.

"I examined the decomposing head of 01ME0639 on May 3, 3002. I took photographs, did a dental autopsy, a dental charting, and took dental radiographs.

I received no dental records for comparison.

The head was that of a child. The dentition was a complete primary dentition with the exception that the mandibular central incisor (O) was missing. The maxillary left central incisor (F) had a DI chip, and the incisors were conical in shape. The roots of the two central and left lateral incisors showed no root resorption. The radiographs showed complete root formation of the primary dentition. The permanent dentition was in the early stages of calcification, with the second premolars and second molars in the bud phases.

If dental records are available and identification is possible. Photographs showing the teeth may provide enough information to make an identification.

In my opinion, based on the development of the permanent teeth, this child is between 3 & 4 years of age."

Her system had no drugs, but blood tests indicated that the child suffered from an infection. Samples of blood spatter on the victim were tested but only indicated that the source was the victim herself. Hinge lifts and fingernail scrapings taken from the body did not reveal anything of significance, nor did anal or vagina swabs, which were negative for semen. However, the vaginal examination indicated internal injuries indicative of sexual assault.

Just inside the skull, the medical examiner found blood clots on the front and right side and another on the left side of her brain. He also found bleeding deeper into the brain, primarily on the left side. She had been violently battered, somehow sustaining a head wound that would prove fatal without medical intervention. He determined she suffered a closed head injury, blunt force trauma, or acceleration/deceleration injury. He ruled it a homicide.

The two black trash bags wrapped around her head were sent to the Royal Canadian Mounted Police Crime Laboratory in Vancouver, British Columbia (B.C.) Canada. They possessed the technology to perform what is known as "vacuum metal deposition" to find fingerprints on materials like the trash bag. The United Kingdom's Home Office developed this testing method to identify perpetrators of the Irish Republic Army bombings that were rampant in the 1970s and 1980s.

With the necessary equipment, VMD is a simple test where evidence—in this case, the black trash bags—is placed in a vacuum chamber, and trace amounts of gold and zinc are heated and vaporized with the metal attaching to any fingerprints that might be present.

Tiny amounts of metal, traditionally gold and zinc, are heated and vaporized. The heavy metals will then attach to any fingerprints that may be present, even if they are not visible to the human eye. Additionally, VMD does not compromise the integrity of DNA that may be present and can be used on evidence that has been exposed to harsh environments, making it a valuable tool for forensic investigators.

The results of the VMD testing came back in January 2002. Unfortunately, no prints could be developed and only smudges were revealed when the process was completed. It was yet another disappointment for the detectives.

A large latex paint chip was discovered in her hair. How a paint chip ended up in her hair would mystify the detectives and send them looking for links to the color and composition to no avail. They had no way of knowing that the paint was picked up post-mortem when her head was first tossed in a dumpster. Her hair samples were sent to an FBI mineralogist for testing. Soil samples were collected from the walkway at the 59th Street residence where Precious Doe lived, the gravel road by the body site, the wooded area where the head was found, and the spaces between where the body parts were found and 59th Street. The results from the FBI Laboratory came back in February 2002. The following is an excerpt from that report.

"The debris includes apparent Portland cement, gypsum, minerals, iron, and apparent charred wood, hairs, and fibers. With the exception of the cobalt-containing

particles, these materials can commonly be found in urban environments. Naturally occurring or manufactured cobalt-containing particles are rare. Portland cement, gypsum, and minerals are frequently used in the manufacture of building materials. Iron is used in the production of many metal objects, from automobiles to nails. Additionally, minerals and iron particles can be found in areas where lead-containing paint, pipes, or solder was used. Strontium-containing particles are produced where road flairs are burned and are found in some fireworks. Charred wood remains as the product of incomplete combustion. Haris (sic) and fibers are found in all inhabited environments.

The materials identified in specimens K1 through K5, soil samples represented as being collected from the area where the victim's body and head were recovered, are unremarkable. The soil present in these areas contains a variety of common minerals."

The report went on to list the minerals identified but concluded, *"Although the debris from the victim's hair contains some materials that are also present in the soil where her body and head were recovered (K1 through K5), the preponderance of the material types found in the debris from her hair was not recovered from the soil. Consequently, the soil is an unlikely source of the debris from the victim's hair."*

The examination and autopsy of the head at least ruled out a serial killer at this point. He determined that the injuries at the origin of where the head was severed matched the injuries found on the torso earlier. It gave the squad a strange sense of relief. With the body parts as a match, it was determined that only one victim existed.

Metal Detectors and Mental Detectors

On the afternoon of May 3, 2001, detectives from the 1020 squad and one from the Overland Park, Kansas Police Department went to the Bulk Mail Center at 4900 Speaker Road to try and interview former work associates of Billy Stegall.

Former work associates of Billy Stegall indicated that he liked to draw attention to himself and would blow the slightest issue out of proportion. That seemed to be the consistent theme amongst all the individuals the detectives spoke to about Stegall. For example, he claimed to be former—sometimes active—military, dressing in camouflage clothing; often, he stated he was a spy working covertly for the CIA and spying on other postal workers; other times, a former security guard. In addition, Stegall would often state he had been in the jungles of Vietnam and tell how he would hide in different places and shoot the Viet Cong.

Although people thought he was crazy and had the potential of "going postal," no one ever saw him at work with a weapon, although he talked about them incessantly. No one ever heard him making any threats to the staff. Instead, they gave descriptions that sounded like something from a cookbook—he was a nut, a flake, a fruitcake.

Everyone shared a consistent impression of how odd but not surprising it was that Stegall had found the victim's head.

Stegall was considered a suspect throughout the early months of the investigation based on all his oddly timed behavior. Because Stegall found the victim's head after insinuating himself into the crime scene, he quickly became a person of interest. As part of the due diligence, Detective Danny Phillips, Kansas City, Missouri Police Homicide Unit, learned that Stegall had contacted the Drug Enforcement Administration (DEA) on April 13, 2001, to report alleged interstate cocaine trafficking. The information he voluntarily provided seemed concocted and sent up red flags with the DEA, resulting in their dismissing Stegall's statements as being without merit. The following is the written communication to Detective Phillips regarding that interaction. Note that all grammatical and spelling errors are from the original documents, not the author's errors.

From: Detective Ed Wisdom, Task Force Officer Kansas Civil District Office. DEA

Subject: Billy Howard Stegall

On 04-13-01, TFO Wisdom received a telephone from Stegall wishing to give information regarding a multi-kilogram distributor of cocaine. TFO Wisdom requested that Stegall come to the Kansas City District Office of the DEA (KCDO) rather than talk over the telephone. TFO Wisdom provided Stegall with directions to the KCDO.

On 04-13-01 at approximately 1:30 P.M., Stegall arrived at the KCDO and was escorted by TFO Wisdom to an interview room. ITO Santiago Vasquez and Group Supervisor Guy Hargreaves also participated in the interview of Stegall

TFO Wisdom learned Stegall lives at XXXX Bales, Kansas City, MO, and resides there with his wife. Stegall stated that he would be able to travel to Atlanta, GA and purchase as much cocaine as he wanted. Stegall stated *that he could buy a kilogram of cocaine in Atlanta for $7,000.00. Stegall stated that he could travel to Key West, FL. But it would cost $13,000.00 because a customs agent was involved. Stegall stated that the cocaine would come from his son Billy Howard Stegall Jr., a black Male, DOB. 09-XX-19XX, telephone number, 770-XXX-XXXX, social security number, XXX-XX-XXXX.*

Stegall stated that his son Stegall, Jr. lived at XXX Walden Drive, Stone Mountain, GA. Stegall stated that Stone Mountain is a suburb of Atlanta, CA. IFO Wisdom asked if Stegall knew his cooperation would result in the arrest and probable imprisonment of his son, and Stegall stated that he did not have a problem doing this to his own son.

Stegall's only concern was that he needed to be armed when the "deal went down". TFO Wisdom explained to Stegall that this was not an option. Stegall stated that he always carried a gun. Stegall stated that his son wanted to bring him into his drug organization because of Stegall's past military experience and his knowledge of weaponry

TFO Wisdom inquired what branch of the service Stegall served. Stegall stated that he served a career in the U.S. Army. Stegall also stated that he was "Rambo" before r±ere was even a "Rambo." Stegall further related that he had served some time in Leavenworth prison for crimes committed in the military but was pardoned by then-Congressman Jimmy Carter. Stegall stated that he served in a special military group in Germany that worked with the German Government.

Stegall stated that while serving in this special group that certain people would use his position to their advantage. TFO Wisdom asked STEGALL to describe an incident. Stegall stated that he was basically undercover and that persons would take him with them to drug transactions. Stegall stated that he would not be able to "bust" these people because they knew who he was.

Stegall returned to requesting a gun again but retracted his statement about needing to carry a gun. Stegall stated that he was a Vietnam veteran, and they could not hurt him anyway because he had a titanium chest.TFO Wisdom inquired what Stegall was meaning. Stegall stated that he bad open heart surgery and the doctor put a titanium plate in his chest. Stegall stated they could shoot him and it wouldn't hurt hirn because he was like "Rambo"

TFO Wisdom stated that he would need to verify the information and would contact him in a few weeks. TFO Wisdom has not contacted Stegall to date as it was deemed that Stegall was unsuitable as a DEA source of information.

The FBI in Quantico developed behaviorally oriented questions for a subsequent interview with Stegall. He grew more reluctant to cooperate and said he wanted Johnny Cochran, O.J. Simpson's lawyer, to represent him if he ever needed an attorney.

While he was being interviewed, other detectives from the squad looked around Stegall's car for anything suspicious in plain view, but nothing was out of the ordinary. After four hours of interviewing, nothing significant was revealed to the detectives. Ultimately, they came back with the best estimate that Stegall didn't have anything to do with the crime. He was just a guy that injected himself into situations that would be better left alone. In the end, Billy Stegall would remain a peculiar character in a story only the gods of mischief could have concocted.

On the morning of May 6, 2001, Sgt. Bernard brought in a team from the Mid-Western Artifacts Society to assist his squad in conducting a field search of the wooded area. Members of a non-profit, incorporated metal detecting club with equipment and specialized resources that the police department did not possess, this team used metal detectors to find any evidence believed to be related to the investigation. They hoped they'd find a knife blade in the ground or some other sharp object that might have been used to decapitate the child. Unfortunately, nothing of any significance was located by the searchers who, like the volunteer K9 teams previously noted, stated it was the roughest brush any of them had ever worked.

This kind of volunteerism and commitment demonstrates the goodness in people and, in situations such as the detectives were facing, it helped bring back some faith in humanity.

The following day, Detectives Phillips and Solomon met with Mike Huscreaux, the Storm Water Superintendent for the Kansas City Water Department at 59th and Kensington. The water department provided a team that, under the direction of Huscreaux, searched the manholes and catch basins in the area between 59th and 61st Streets from Swope Parkway to Manchester in the hope of finding evidence related to the homicide. The storm drains and sewer lines in that area drained into a four-foot pipe at the lowest point at 59th and Kensington, the area closest to where the body was found. From that point, running water would travel to an interceptor before dumping into a creek at 58th Street. Nothing of any significance was located in the portions that water employees could access. The southernmost part of the pipeline was inaccessible due to a high amount of water running through it. Huscreaux advised officers that if an object were placed in the manhole nearest that location, it would have been washed away further down the line in the direction of the sewage treatment plant or into the runoff, which dumps into the creek at 58th Street. Due to the extreme amount of water pressure in the storm sewers, recovery of anything of value would be virtually impossible.

How It All Started

On the morning of May 31, 2001, detectives were sent to a home on East 59th Street to make contact with a potential witness named Albert Morton to learn what, if anything, he may have seen or heard on the night of April 28th, 2001. No one answered the door, but they noticed a man fitting Morton's description standing at the "Precious Doe" memorial at 59th and Kensington on the southwest corner. It was indeed Albert Morton, so the detectives started a conversation regarding why they were there. Mr. Morton stated that he had seen a friend at 59th Street and Elmwood and had engaged in conversation. "Mr. Macey," as he described him, was an elderly gentleman who resided at 59th Street and Elmwood and he had been out for a walk with his unleashed dog. After a brief conversation, Morton headed back to his own home and, at some point, noticed Macey following him. As he considered Macey to be somewhat senile, he (Morton) redirected Macey back to the direction of his home and then proceeded on toward his original destination.

After stopping to visit with another friend, Albert Morton looked back and didn't see Macey again but saw Macey's dog walking northbound on the access road at 59th and Kensington into the wooded area. Concerned that his friend might have wandered into the woods, Morton went to the access road at 59th and Kensington northbound into the wooded area to try and find Macey. He walked north on the road to a clearing where he saw trash and an old washing machine and dryer in the clearing. He saw the dog and got him to follow him back down the road to 59th Street, but the dog turned and headed back into the woods. Morton once again followed the dog and got him to come with him back to 59th Street. He stated that he never saw the victim in the woods and that the dog never behaved in any way that indicated that he had detected it. He said that soon after leaving the area, he met up with Mrs. Macey, who revealed her husband never came home, so Morton called the police. He thought it was about 6:30 p.m. That's all he remembered.

All Roads Lead to Nowhere

Sgt. Bernard asked the KCPD's Information Technology Department to create a computer-generated database to collect and share the information to manage all the leads pouring in. First, a lead sheet was used by whoever took the call. Then, that information was inputted into a database and prioritized by one of three categories: A) immediate, B) later, and C) never, providing an organized method of sifting through all the information logically.

Steve McBride was the field representative for the Center for Missing and Exploited Children. He sent photos of the head to their headquarters so that a computer-generated composite could be developed. It was a beautiful picture, but this first rendition of the "Do You Know Me?" poster revealed a child whose face looked too old to be a preschooler. In this picture, the child had clothes on, braided hair, and an earring in the ear, which Precious Doe didn't have. It was lovely and lifelike, but not her. Flyers with this picture were produced, including her height, weight, estimated age, and the identifying feature of the crescent-shaped birthmark on her shoulder.

Volunteers from the Ad Hoc Group Against Crime passed out flyers. Kansas City's Ad Hoc Group Against Crime was initially formed in the late 1970s to mobilize resources to help solve the murders of nine African American women and has since become a resource for the community and law enforcement. One of its missions is to bring justice to crime victims and nowhere was there a more pressing need for justice than in the case of Precious Doe. Her likeness was everywhere. Grocery stores, shopping malls, light posts—the image of Precious Doe was everywhere but getting someone to identify her went nowhere. So Ad Hoc established a secret witness hotline. The KCPD used the Crimestoppers TIPS hotline and a reward fund was started. The FBI gave $15,000 toward the reward fund. This addition increased the reward to $33,000, but there were no takers.

Even in the earliest days of the investigation, frustration was high. Detectives and the medical examiner agreed that, while the composite of Precious Doe that the Center for Missing Children generated was well done, it did not reflect the actual victim. The medical examiner pointed out numerous discrepancies and a local forensic artist was brought in to produce drawings utilizing the real autopsy photos as a reference.

Someone gave the name and address of the alleged suspect to the secret witness hotline and members of Ad Hoc were going to go after the guy. No matter how egregious the crime was, no group could be allowed to take matters into their own hands and the police interceded in that one. The named individual didn't have any connection to the case and an unfortunate incident was averted. Whoever the accused individual was, he didn't know just how lucky he was. There were countless random items of clothing found by residents near the scene. These would be turned in to the police hoping that something might be related. Every week and every new tip resulted in some excitement on the part of the detectives. Emotions ran high and then low, but the leads were all dead-ends.

Who Are You?

The staff at the Jackson County Medical Examiner's office suggested that Frank Bender be contacted to see if he would do a reconstruction of Precious Doe's head from her skull. Bender was a nationally known sculptor who succeeded with reconstructions that resulted in identifying deceased individuals and aiding in clearing missing persons and homicide cases. Bender agreed to take on the project for $1,800 and flew to Kansas City to pick up Precious Doe's skull and take it back for reconstruction. Before Bender's arrival, the head needed to be prepared, so mealworms were used to eat the flesh off the bones. There is no dignity in violent death. It exposes the victim in ways unimaginable, right down to the bare bone. The "big reveal" of Bender's re-creation was done in Kansas City on August 31, 2001. The Jackson County prosecutor's office had a trailer set up for the press conference where Bender was introduced and the bust of Precious Doe was unveiled. There were audible gasps of "Oh, my God" from the onlookers as her image was shown for the first time. It was a far cry from the photos of the decapitated head that had been so carelessly tossed aside.

The press conference gained national network attention, and the case was featured on the *Today Show* on Labor Day morning. Photos of the bust and fingerprints were issued, and the flyer was posted on Interpol in October 2001. An inquiry came from London authorities regarding an African American male whose unidentified body had been discarded in the River Thames in September 2001. Mitochondrial DNA was performed on that victim and comparisons were requested to determine if there might be some common denominator in those crimes. It was a stretch, but the Precious Doe case had reached out across oceans in search of any possible clues to identify this little girl, no matter how small. It was evident that detectives in the United Kingdom were as anxious to solve their child murder case as the Kansas City detectives; however, science would prove that these were unrelated deaths.

Five months after Precious Doe's body was discovered, police were contacted from halfway around the world about a decapitated Black male approximately the same age as Kansas City's unnamed child in an attempt to determine if there was a possible connection. On September 21, 2001, the little boy's mutilated torso was found floating in the River Thames near Tower Bridge in central London. Dubbed "Adam" by police officers, the unidentified remains belonged to a black male, around four to eight years old, wearing a pair of orange girls' shorts. The label was printed in German and marketed under "Kids & Company." That single clue would be significant in narrowing down individuals connected with the child's disappearance.

The autopsy indicated Adam was poisoned and his throat had been slit to drain the blood from his body. There were no signs of physical or sexual abuse, and he was well-nourished. His head and limbs had been painstakingly removed before he was thrown into the river, where it appeared he had been for approximately ten days.

Two different plants were found in Adam's stomach contents. One was the Calabar bean, named for Old Calabar, an eastern province of Nigeria, where it is grown. It is also called the Doomsday or ordeal plant and is used in African witchcraft ceremonies. The amount found in Adam's autopsy would have resulted in paralysis of his nervous system but would still allow him to be awake. The other foreign contents were from the Datura plant, an invasive, noxious weed common in Africa. It is a hallucinogenic that possesses some sedative effects. The fact that Adam would have been aware of his throat being cut presented a horrific scenario for detectives to process.

The forensic examiners found that the child had ingested a burned mixture containing ground bone, clay, and minute amounts of gold and quartz along with the plants. This combination was similar to ingredients used in African rituals. Traces of cough syrup were also found in his stomach, possibly given to make the concoction more palatable. It was suspected that Adam was trafficked to London to be used in a muti killing, a ritual sacrifice performed by a witch doctor. The child would be killed and the body parts used to make "black magic" or medicinal potions called "muti," which would explain why Adam's head and limbs were never recovered.

The evidence pointed to a human sacrifice conducted in the method of Yoruban rituals that originated in Nigeria, so local soil and mineral samples were obtained from that area for comparison with the contents found in Adam's body. A sophisticated testing method that archeologists had primarily utilized was now being applied to forensic investigations but had only been used in rare instances. Stable isotope testing was conducted to determine the geographical origin of the victim. Based on the contents of the child's stomach and the makeup of his bones, it was determined that he had most likely come from a town in southwestern Nigeria where voodoo was commonplace. Furthermore, the pollen tests on stomach contents confirmed he had only been in London for a short time before he was murdered.

A search of international missing children databases raised many leads, but nothing to match the little boy found in London. Investigators were worried that the worldwide reaction to the September 11th terrorist attacks overshadowed the case. They worked to garner as much publicity as possible in the hope that someone would provide helpful information about the victim's identity. A reward fund was established to try and create interest in the story and garner leads that might prove beneficial.

Because of the link to Africa, authorities reached out to Nelson Mandela, former President of South Africa, who publicly requested assistance from the African community for help in identifying the child. His statement, translated into tribal languages, was broadcast across the continent. "Scotland Yard informs me that early indications of their investigations are that the boy comes from somewhere in Africa, so if anywhere, even in the remotest village of our continent, there is a family missing a son of that age who might have disappeared around that time... please contact the police."

The following year, London authorities physically followed leads in Nigeria, traveling anywhere that might have helpful information regarding the case, but nothing proved successful.

In July 2002, social workers in Glasgow became worried about the safety of two little girls living with their mother, a Nigerian woman in her early 30s who had relocated from Germany. Her name was Joyce Osagiede. The woman claimed to be a refugee fleeing from a Yoruba cult and that her family was in danger, describing human sacrifices and murders. When they checked on the children's welfare, the caseworkers found items related to rituals in Osagiede's apartment and notified law enforcement. One of the officers responding to the call saw a possible connection to Adam's case and informed the London investigators.

Detectives searched Joyce's home and found clothes with the same "Kids & Company" label and in the exact sizes as Adam's orange shorts. She had no plausible explanation for the potentially damning evidence and was arrested. When news of the arrest was released to the media, a German social worker came forward, stating she had handled a benefits claim for Joyce Osagiede in 2001 in Hamburg. She indicated the woman had two daughters and was also accompanied by a small boy, but Osagiede was not attempting to apply for financial aid for him. The child she described appeared to be fearful and withdrawn. She stated the woman treated the child as an inconvenience, clutching him tightly as if she feared he would run away. She reported the information to the police when she realized she might have been the last person to see Adam alive.

Forensic testing traced Adam's birthplace to an area around Benin City in southern Nigeria—Joyce Osagiede's hometown—further bolstering the potential case against her. Still, police were never able to charge her with a crime. She was, however, deported back to Nigeria.

Surveillance of the woman's associates brought the police to another Nigerian, a man named Kingsley Ojo. By July 2003, details from police surveillance allowed them to build a case against Ojo and almost two dozen other human traffickers. A search of Ojo's residence uncovered items related to rituals, including videos, one of which showed the beheading of an adult. Still, no DNA evidence linking him to Adam was found. Nevertheless, Ojo was convicted on four counts of trafficking and served four years in jail before being deported back to Nigeria. He was never charged with the death of Adam.

A year after the child's body was discovered, a memorial service was conducted in London to honor the unidentified little boy now known in the United Kingdom as Adam. The refusal to allow missing children like Adam and Precious Doe to go unnamed seemed a common thread that spanned the globe to connect little lost souls. The small gathering consisted of law enforcement and scientific community members who worked so diligently to solve this case. Yet, like Precious Doe, it seemed that the only ones stepping up to mourn him were caring strangers who knew him only in death but placed a value on his short life. It was a family formed by tragedy.

As part of the international investigation, German police learned that Joyce had lived in Hamburg until late 2001—the city where the orange shorts found on Adam's body were bought. They also recovered property she had left behind with a friend and uncovered photographs, including one dated 2001—the eerie image of a small boy about five years old staring directly at the camera.

In early 2011, Joyce Osagiede said that Adam was indeed the boy in the photograph found in Germany and his real name was Ikpomwosa. She said she had given him to a man called Bawa, but authorities could never positively identify him. Osagiede also named an individual pictured in another photograph that was recovered. The person she named Bawa was the man law enforcement knew as Kingsley Ojo the convicted human trafficker. Still, no evidence could link Ojo directly to Adam's disappearance or death.

A quarter century after the child's body was found floating in the River Thames, some 4,300 miles from home, no one has been brought to justice for Adam's death. Joyce Osagiede is now deceased and Kingsley Ojo is believed to be somewhere in Nigeria.

Another missing child submitted as a lead was the case of Rilya Wilson, an African American child missing from Florida. Dirk Tarpley hoped this might be the lead that took them to Precious Doe, encouraged by the prospect that she might be identified. But unfortunately Sgt. Bernard insisted it wasn't her. He couldn't give a reason other than his gut telling him "no," and he was ultimately proved correct. Nevertheless, he was plowing forward, looking for the identity of Kansas City's little girl lost.

Rilya Shenise Wilson was approximately four years old when she disappeared from the foster care system in Florida on January 18, 2001. However, it was not 15 months later that the little girl was determined to be missing from her foster home, where she and her younger sister lived with Geralyn Graham and her partner, Pamela Kendrick, aka Pamela Graham. On April 18, 2002, a new caseworker assigned to the children by the Florida Department of Children and Families (DCF) discovered that Rilya was not living there. Geralyn claimed that someone from the agency had picked up Rilya for an evaluation and that Rilya never returned.

She also insisted that another DCF worker had come to the house a few weeks later to gather Rilya's clothes and toys. In actuality, Pamela and Geralyn had sold the child's bed and belongings at a garage sale, safe in the knowledge that the child would no longer be needing those. However, she could not explain why she never inquired about the child or where she had been placed. Graham had even gone so far as to falsify Rilya's vaccination records in 2001 after the child disappeared to continue receiving state benefits for the child's care. Graham was later jailed for identity fraud and Medicaid fraud for accepting payments on behalf of Rilya after she went missing.

Her claim about DCF taking the child was quickly disproved as the investigation into Rilya's case expanded. What was discovered, however, was that her previous social worker, Deborah Muskelly, had falsified her reports and failed to check on the children assigned to her. Instead, Muskelly worked as a substitute teacher when she was supposed to conduct in-person foster care visits. Muskelly was eventually charged with forty-one criminal charges related to her position at the Florida Department of Children and Families (DCF), including grand theft. When she pled guilty to one count of official misconduct, the other charges against her were dropped. However, she was placed on probation and ordered never to work with children or for the government again. Muskelly was never charged with any crime related to Rilya's disappearance. Because of the mishandling of Rilya's case, both Muskelly's supervisor and the director of DCF were forced to resign their positions.

In the Rilya Wilson case, it was learned that she and her younger sister were placed in the home after her mother, Gloria Wilson, lost custody of her children because of her cocaine abuse. Conflicting stories were given about the possibility of Rilya being Graham's niece, granddaughter, or having some other biological relationship, but none of these were ever substantiated. In addition, Gloria Wilson had named multiple men as possibly being Rilya's biological father, but there were never any state-ordered DNA tests conducted on any of those individuals.

Geralyn Graham moved to Miami in 1994 with her partner, Pamela Kendrick. The two women were not related or married despite often using the same last name. In 1999, the couple met Gloria Wilson, Rilya's mother. Wilson, a drug addict, was pregnant with Rilya's younger sister. Because of her drug use, Wilson surrendered her parental rights when her baby was born. DCF placed the girls in the temporary custody of non-relative adults, Geralyn Graham and Pamela Kendrick. Graham had used 42 aliases in multiple states and was convicted of food stamp fraud in Tennessee a decade earlier. She was still on probation in Florida for those crimes, but the woman was still deemed acceptable to foster children in that state.

Rilya did not adjust well to her new environment, frustrating Graham, who began to abuse the child. Graham would later state to authorities that she did not feel she was paid enough to care for the child and wanted the state to take her back. She indicated that DCF did not want to separate the child and denied the request, although no records existed that substantiated Graham's claims.

Authorities removed Rilya's younger sister from Graham's home shortly after discovering that one of the Wilson children was missing. Despite the investigation underway, Graham insisted that the child was safe with her. Taking the child out of her home would result in Graham losing state funds and she resisted that vehemently. However, a judge ruled that Rilya's younger sister was neglected, citing the little girl's developmental problems and a health issue that needed medical attention. In addition, both Graham and Kendrick failed multiple lie detector tests regarding Rilya's disappearance, resulting in their arrests.

Pamela Kendrick testified against Graham at her trial, claiming that both of them had spanked Rilya with switches and had locked her in a dog cage, which prosecutors produced as evidence for the jury to consider. In addition, she described an incident in which Rilya suffered severe burns from the water heater in the small laundry room where the child was forced to stay, only being allowed to leave to use the bathroom. Finally, Kendrick noted that Graham refused to take the little girl for medical care despite Kendrick's suggestion that it be sought.

In August 2004, Graham was finally charged with kidnapping as defined by Florida statutes, along with three counts of child abuse. Kendrick, charged with two lesser counts of child abuse/neglect, vehemently denied any involvement in Rilya's disappearance but confessed to abusing the child. She also admitted that she had known since December of 2000 that Graham was making up the story about the DCF worker coming to take Rilya. Kendrick agreed to testify against Graham in exchange for days in prison, followed by five years probation.

In March 2005, Graham was additionally charged with the first-degree murder of Rilya Wilson. Kendrick and other witnesses stated that Graham had admitted to smothering Rilya. Several individuals testified that Graham had told a story about an unnamed Spanish woman who wanted to adopt Rilya and took her for a visit; sometimes the story was that they went to New York and other times it was New Jersey. When authorities noted the conflicting reports, she said the woman brought Rilya back and that DCF took her away shortly after that. None of the versions ever matched, and none could be corroborated, but the one constant was that each witness had heard a similar version of Graham's explanation for why the child was gone.

The tale she told about an unknown Hispanic woman taking the child was eerily similar to another missing child investigation in Florida, the 2008 Caylee Anthony case. In that disappearance, the child's mother, Casey Anthony, claimed her missing daughter had been left in the care of her nanny, Zenaida Fernandez-Gonzalez, whom she referred to as Zanny the Nanny at the time of her disappearance. However, during her murder trial, Casey Anthony would ultimately admit that she made up the story.

Witnesses testified that Graham claimed to have disposed of the body in a canal near her home, believing "no body, no murder" would keep her from being found guilty of anything related to the missing child. She also insisted that the child was "evil" and needed to be killed because she refused to wear an angel costume for Halloween.

Graham's trial took place twelve years after Rilya was discovered missing. The jury convicted Graham of kidnapping and child abuse but deadlocked 11-to-1 on the murder because Rilya's body had not been recovered. The judge declared a mistrial on the murder charges and Graham was sentenced to 55 years in prison for the other crimes.

In January 2013, the jury convicted Graham of kidnapping and aggravated child abuse but deadlocked 11-to-1 on the charge of murder. As a result, the judge sentenced 67-year-old Graham to 30 years for the kidnapping plus 25 years for aggravated child abuse, to be served consecutively. In theory, the number of years was a life sentence for the woman who misplaced the child who was erroneously placed in her custody.

Although Rilya's first name is an acronym for "really I love you always," she disappeared unloved and unlocated. To date, her body has never been found.

After Rilya Wilson, there was another near miss with a little missing girl named Brittany Renee Williams. Unfortunately, the child in Kansas City wasn't Brittany, either. How many missing children are out there? It was mind-boggling.

Brittany Williams' mother gave guardianship to a woman named Kim E. Parker shortly before she succumbed to AIDS. Parker allegedly ran a charity for children with serious health issues. However, the not-for-profit organization, Rainbow Kids, was actually a fraudulent operation with the sole purpose of collecting Social Security and Medicaid funds for the children in her care. In addition, Parker had been reported for abuse and neglect on multiple occasions.

Brittany Williams was small for her age because she contracted AIDS from her mother before she was born. The last documented contact with the child was an August 2000 visit to her doctor as part of her ongoing health issues. During that visit, it was noted that Brittany's hair had been cut very short due to head lice. She required significant care due to her medical condition; an issue that frustrated Parker. She told Brittany's adult half-sister that the child "had lived longer" than she expected when she took her as a foster child and tried to persuade her to take the little girl. Unfortunately, the sister could not care for the critically ill child and turned Parker down. When the sister indicated that she wanted to remain in contact with Brittany, Parker stated that the child was being placed with two female friends but refused to offer any additional details.

In the Fall of 2000, authorities arrested Parker for failing to send Brittany to school. Charges were dismissed when Parker told the court she no longer had custody, but no one bothered to verify her story. Had the court looked into the case, it would have been discovered that the child was missing and that Parker continued to receive financial benefits for the little girl.

The following year, Parker was called back before the same judge for failing to obtain a court-ordered paternity test needed to try and place the child with biological family members. But, again, nothing was followed up on, and no one thought to ask Parker to produce the child. In the meantime, Parker was collecting funds intended for Brittany, using the monies to renovate her house.

Parker continued to defy court orders, and finally, in January 2003, her guardianship of Brittany was revoked and reassigned to Virginia social services. When caseworkers could not locate the child, law enforcement was called to open an investigation, but Parker refused to cooperate with authorities. As a result, she was held in contempt of court and jailed. At this time, her story of the two friends taking Brittany was disproved, and the search for Brittany continued. As detectives delved into Parker's business dealings, the fraud she perpetrated on donors to her organization and the illegal use of welfare funds came to light. In April 2003, Parker faced over 70 felony charges, and Her Rainbow Kids' pot of gold was finally emptied.

Detectives conducted a massive search of Parker's residence, its septic system, and the property itself, but nothing related to Brittany's possible death was discovered. She was still considered a missing child, but the lack of activity on her Medicaid card and Social Security number painted a grim image. Without constant medical care and medications, the little girl was most likely deceased.

Finally, in December of that year, Parker received a federal prison sentence for fraud, with the judge handing down the maximum sentence of eight years. An additional two-year sentence was given to Parker by the state of Virginia when she was tried for Medicaid fraud. Parker was never charged with the death of Brittany Williams.

The detectives chased leads from people who made up stories about the crime to gain attention. "A white man in a hardware store with a little black girl." He was described as "mean to the girl, (sic) and he bought a machete." It never happened, but the squad had no way of knowing that, so they ran it down anyway. Daylight burned away and left little more than dashed hope and ashes.

An informant told the story of a house she knew about where Precious Doe was killed. She claimed that she'd been in the place where the murder occurred. She described a secret attic room where the child had taken chalk and written the alphabet in chalk on one of the walls and said you had to go through a bedroom and into the closet where a hidden panel could be found. It was access to the attic space. She said the child was kept in shackles and killed on a mattress soaked in blood. The lead was followed, and the detectives located the house. It was vacant and in the process of being rehabbed. The owner permitted officers to search the house. Frank Booth, a team of crime scene technicians, and detectives conducted the search. The hidden panel in the closet on the second floor was located where she said it was, and the investigative team thought this was it. When it was opened, a stained mattress was found and there was childish writing on one wall. There were no shackles, but the mattress looked promising. Frank Booth tested the mattress for blood. No reaction. It may have been paint or varnish but not blood. No blood was found anywhere. The house held a tale to tell, but it wasn't Precious Doe's story.

Someone also reported a guy in jail who described decapitating a child in the attic of a house. His details were so vivid and convincing that a search warrant was obtained. Maybe something happened there long ago—perhaps his memories of being locked in the attic himself as a child—but Precious Doe didn't die there. No one did. The squad chased down scores of leads of children being abused. There were hundreds of them. The children were always located, but who knew if they would eventually end up like Doe?

Then there was the issue of all the missing kids across the country that fit her description. How many disposable children are there? Is it a national phenomenon? Over and over, the leads were run down. The members of the 1020 Squad were beginning to get run down from exhaustion and disappointment. Finally, *America's Most Wanted* featured the little unnamed girl. The story of Precious Doe was so compelling that *Cold Case Files* also featured it, even though it was an unsolved case. Unfortunately, the one major daytime show they hoped would feature it declined, as the producer wasn't interested in pursuing this story.

We Commit Your Soul

On December 8, 2001, Precious Doe was buried for the first time. Her clothing was lovingly donated by members of a grassroots group that formed and called itself the "Precious Doe Committee." This group would become active in this case and others where advocates were needed for the cause. They are beautiful souls who claimed this little child as their own. Over 1,000 people attended the service at the Metropolitan Missionary Baptist Church. This was the first of several services that the church members would participate in for her. Precious Doe was buried in a white casket with a pink burial vault. She was laid to rest at Memorial Park Cemetery in a grave donated by Richard Childs, one of the Memorial Park executives. With his many years in the funeral business, dealing with gruesome deaths was not foreign to him, and he understood what law enforcement had seen and lived with daily. They were kin in the Brotherhood of Death.

There was concern about a potential for a tug of war over the child's remains, such as they were, should someone come forward to claim her. In a preemptive strike, the Precious Doe Committee, with the help of city council members, petitioned the court for an order that her remains would remain where they belonged—in Kansas City. She was already in the community's hearts and minds and she needed to stay here where she at least had a loving family in the afterlife. Because of the notoriety the case brought, the Precious Doe Committee requested a declaratory judgment to maintain custody of the deceased child under the court's oversight so that the body's final disposition would require judicial oversight. It further suggested that the outcome be either the eventual return of the child to relatives, based upon evidence to that effect, or permanent rest at Memorial Park Cemetery, where she was initially interred in December 2001. As fate would have it, she would be allowed to remain there but not until long after the case was solved.

Life is a Granola Bowl – Lots of Nuts and Flakes

Strange leads came in from everywhere. Based on the number of sightings, Precious Doe traveled to more cities than Flat Stanley. Scores of people with visions, dreams, and ideas about the case called the hotline. Each call was logged and followed up on by the squad. Finally, in July 2002, a psychic called the Homicide Unit and stated that she had been talking with Precious Doe for the last six months and was speaking to her. She passed on the following bits and pieces of information taken directly from the case file:

1. *The letters "I.K."*
2. *The words "O'baya, O'Be, O'Bomba."*
3. *"A tall man with gray salt and pepper hair with a long stick knows more than what he's told."*
4. *"Precious Doe was taken to an Asian store with a star on top of it."*
5. *"Spanish witchcraft."*
6. *"Not that much blood in her body."*
7. *"Hung upside down."*
8. *"Mother from California."*
9. *"White stucco two-story house."*

10. *"Brought from California, Precious Doe was drunk or drugged all the way here."*
11. *"3 chops to the head."*
12. *"Big building, there was an alter (sic) in it."*
13. *"Man has three piercings in his ears and short hair."*
14. *"Man fondled Precious Doe."*
15. *"Precious Doe's blood used for some other purpose."*
16. *"Mothers (sic) name is Bessie, and she is dead."*
17. *"The name of "Maria" as Precious Doe's name, possibly with Hispanic blood in her."*
18. *"Precious Doe had a bag with her mothers (sic) picture in it.. (sic)"*
19. *"The bag was thrown away."*
20. *"They ran from California to be here."*
21. *"The man got a traffic ticket here."*
22. *"The man has high cheekbones."*
23. *"Precious Doe kept repeating, "House near me."*
24. *"He felt guilty."*
25. *"He or someone connected with him put the head, where it was found, afterwards (sic)."*
26. *"The head was supposed to go into the water."*
27. *"Older woman saw Precious Doe being removed from the building."*
28. *The woman that witnessed Precious Doe's removal drives a blue in color "Falcon."*
29. *"Precious Doe hears singing."*
30. *"Precious Doe's body was, where it was discovered, for 3 to 5 days before it was discovered."*
31. *"Precious Doe has no living relatives."*

32. *"Precious Doe's mother is dead or was killed where drugs were involved."*
33. *"The man that brought Precious Doe to Kansas City is no longer in Kansas City, and he had come to Kansas City with a female who was wearing all white."*
34. *"The names "Joe", "JM", and "Jaro" are possibly the names of the male who brought Precious Doe to Kansas City."*
35. *"Tranquilizers were in Precious Does system, possibly natural herbs."*
36. *"Precious Doe's head was 10 feet away from her body."*
37. *"Precious Doe was reporting that she "saw" green buttons, a green shirt, and a man with salt and pepper hair with a mustache and a big stick."*
38. *"There was no blood in the house where the man with the salt and pepper hair lives."*
39. *"The man with the salt and pepper hair had a house with a carport or garage attached to the house."*
40. *"Precious Doe was unconscious when she was killed"*
41. *"25W" is talked about with relation to the corner store with the star on it."*
42. *"The store was a grocery store."*
43. *"Precious Doe was taken to that store to buy candy and food."*
44. *"Precious Doe was locked up a lot."*
45. *"Precious Doe liked Bugs Bunny."*
46. *"4 rows."*
47. *"1 block away...white house...man with bad stick...3 or 4 steps up...porch...white stucco...2 story."*
48. *"3 or 4 chops...not an axe...possibly a machete or sword...ritual."*

49. *"Vision of a pink nightgown"*
50. *"Precious Doe was drugged up when killed."*
51. *"Precious Doe reports being in a room, with a fenced yard, looking out the window in Kansas City."*
52. *"Precious Doe was brought to that house at night."*
53. *"Precious Doe was brought to Kansas City in a van with California plates 3 to 4 weeks before she was murdered."*
54. *"Building...drove a long way."*
55. *"Barn...alter (sic)...singing."*
56. *"Dressed in pure white gown."*
57. *"Bedsheet."*
58. *"Marks on legs.*
59. *"Held upside down."*
60. *"Heard bag placed by man with stick."*
61. *"Stick, he might not have done it, but he knew about it."*
62. *"Precious Doe never went to school."*
63. *"Precious Doe only went to a Doctor (sic) in California."*
64. *"Medicaid...Calimed (sic)."*
65. *"Doe was born in California."*
66. *"Almost 6 ½ years old" When asked to clarify if that meant at the time of the murder or at the time of the report, the caller stated she could not obtain that information).*
67. *"Born in cold month, killed in hot month."*.
68. *"Loves rivers and oceans."*
69. *"Could walk from house in California to the river or ocean.*
70. *"25th West."*
71. *"She has nobody, (sic) and she is sad."*

72. *"Wax under her fingernails."*
73. *"Her tummy hurts."*
74. *"Something happened to her bones."*
75. *"Sexual fondling with fingers."*
76. *"Bones hurt."*
77. *"Mother was going to take her to a play auntie, but her mother left her with the killer."*

After providing this subconscious salad of a little of this and that, she stated she'd lost contact with Precious Doe but talked to her all the time. The detective asked her to get Precious Doe to tell her what her name was and who her mother was, but the psychic said that Precious Doe wasn't giving it to her. She then offered another bit of information. "I know this sounds weird, but I have a ghost in my car right now that I have to take to the graveyard. He appears in my car once in a while, and I take him back to the graveyard." The detective told her to call back if she got more helpful information. But, of course, one can only speculate if he told her to make sure that "Casper" buckled his seatbelt.

The Price for the Ferryman's Ride

Research shows that stress causes 80-85% of all human illnesses and diseases. In criminal justice-related occupations, the body's circadian rhythm is continually disrupted due to the erratic types of shift work. For example, the Homicide Unit included a shift called Murder Squad, a polite name for "overworked detectives dying on their feet," where they were the first responders to any suspicious death where there was no known suspect. Sometimes they'd work 72 hours straight with no downtime, no sleep, and no real meals—just some mystery meat sandwich out of the vending machine at Police Headquarters or a stale cookie discovered in the recesses of a desk drawer. It was less-than-fine dining for Kansas City's finest. The risk factors for heart disease, cancer, and other health issues are significantly higher in this profession. Divorce, suicide, alcohol abuse—these rates are all increased. There is a documented loss of memory, lack of concentration, depression, and burnout. Post-traumatic stress is high, but it goes unrecognized in this line of work. It is considered a sign of weakness rather than the stress-related physiological outcome of an erratic work schedule, the pressures felt for lack of closure on cases, and the continual slopping through bodily fluids, fleas, cockroaches, unimaginable filth, and gore.

Family members suffer from "spillover" stress. The cascade effects of burnout, depersonalization, intense cynicism, suspiciousness, physical ailments, and other relationship difficulties officers experience have a huge and lasting impact on their personal lives and social interactions. In addition, the pressures and demands of the detective's job result in being "missing in action" for much of anything outside the realm of gruesome crime scenes.

Here's an example: Sgt. Bernard was called out and had to deal with an infant death before he could go to the hospital for the birth of his first grandchild. Death clearly took precedence over life, and this was another one of those outlandish examples of the twisted way we dealt with life in the Homicide Unit. Detectives were involuntary riders on a runaway train, destination unknown. The impact on police families from this indirect involvement with violent crime is significant and it causes stress all its own. It leaves the spouse, significant other, or children—whoever is critical in the officer's life—out on their own for holidays, school programs, PTA and scout meetings, and most other major events. Sometimes, even the basics go begging. Yet, Sgt. Bernard maintained a stoic facade and internalized the stress and exhaustion pressure in his eyes and face. His linebacker-sized shoulders seemed to be a little less straight, but he kept putting one foot in front of the other.

The one thing that he continued to do was his photography. He is a fantastic photographer, and his specialty is nature photography. He captures the beauty of anything outdoors, whether animal, vegetable, or mineral. Perhaps this is how he kept his sanity. Despite all the horrific scenes and unspeakable acts of violence he came to know, he never lost sight of what is beautiful in the world, providing a salve for the mental wounds he endured. When focusing the camera lens on the details of a butterfly's wing, you can think of nothing else.

If ghastly images and mental monsters were chasing him, he was scooped up like a child, protected by Mother Nature. T'was beauty that killed those beasts.

At the scene of an accident, officers call for an immediate medical response. Unfortunately, the Precious Doe case was a train wreck, with all the relationships, life events, and slivers of normalcy being derailed, and no emotional first aid was ever offered. For the1020 Squad, normal was just a setting on the clothes dryer.

The Doll

A *Law and Order: SVU* episode aired on November 8, 2002, called "Dolls." It had the obligatory caution that followed the opening credits: "The following is fictional and does not depict any actual person or event."

This particular storyline depicted detectives working a case involving a murdered little girl that had all the markings of the Precious Doe case. It was not difficult to follow the script and predict how this would play out. In 60 minutes, minus 30 minutes of commercials, my favorites, Stabler and Benson, would solve this case and save the next potential victim. It was like a Reader's Digest version of the Precious Doe case but with one caveat. They solved it within days.

Of course, this just added to the level of public expectations. If fictional New York detectives could knock this out of the ballpark, why couldn't Kansas City detectives and the FBI do the same? One could only imagine what phone calls the 1020 squad was fielding when this was broadcasted. But, unfortunately, back in Kansas City, the search for the identity of Precious Doe offered no light at the end of a tunnel that felt like a coal chute to Hell.

Arts and Sciences

In 2003, Lee Hammond, an Overland Park artist and illustrator, produced a set of drawings based on the actual face of the deceased child. Hammond's chillingly accurate portraits drew a great deal of local attention, but no identification came forward as a result of her work. Then, in October 2003, Sgt. Bernard requested permission to use a private DNA lab in Sarasota, Florida, to test the ethnic origins of Precious Doe. A specialized testing method could provide the percentages of an individual's genetic make-up within four possible groups: Sub-Saharan African, Native American, East Asian, and European. In addition, it could further drill down European ancestry into more specific subgroups: Northwestern European, Southeastern European, Middle Eastern, and South Asian. The company, DNAPrint Genomics, was referred to him by his good friend, Susanne Stiltner, from the FBI's Violent Criminal Apprehension Program (VICAP).

The Louisiana Multi-Agency Homicide Task Force (comprised of the FBI and multiple law enforcement agencies, including the Baton Rouge and Breaux Bridge police departments) had recently used them on a case where they identified the biogeographical ancestry of a serial killer with African American and Native American ancestry. The test was a match for the killer when he was caught. In that case, Derrick Todd Lee, the Louisiana serial killer, had just been successfully identified utilizing the technology. It was initially believed that the serial killer's profile was that of a Caucasian male based on what proved to be mistaken eyewitness accounts. However, the testing of DNA from multiple crime scenes indicated that the suspect was 85% Sub-Saharan African and 15% Native American. Lee had been considered a person of interest early in the investigation and was successfully apprehended based on the scientific results. Both John Wilson and Frank Booth from the KCPD Crime Lab agreed that this testing was valid, and a request for BioGeographical Ancestry analysis (BGA) went up the chain of command for approval. The sample was a blood standard from Precious Doe and was sent for testing. Two months later, the results were in, and it was determined that the victim was 60% Sub-Saharan African and 40% Indo-European descent, with zero percentages of East Asian or Native American ancestry. As it turned out, Precious Doe's maternal grandmother was Caucasian and her grandfather was African American. Old-fashioned investigative techniques confirmed what we had learned of Precious Doe's heredity through modern science.

In the summer of 2003, Precious Doe's body was to be exhumed. The first time she was buried, the court order to keep her in Kansas City was signed. Therefore, it was necessary to have Alvin Brooks and the committee members go back and ask that the court vacate that order and issue an order for exhumation so that a forensic team could re-access the body for further identification so that the investigation could continue. On July 15, 2003, a search warrant signed by Jackson County, Missouri Circuit Court Judge Jay Daugherty was served at Memorial Park Cemetery for the exhumation of Precious Doe's coffin to seize evidence which, in this case, was her body and head. The FBI funded the expenses incurred to accomplish this as it would require the retrieval of the child's remains and the re-burial at a later date. Detective Eric Dillenkoffer served the warrant and CST Melissa Thompson responded to photograph the scene.

With the help of Rick Childs and Park Lawn Cemetery, the body was disinterred, the process taking approximately an hour for removal of the coffin and then its contents. Dillenkoffer took official custody of the evidence described in the warrant—Precious Doe's head and body—subsequently turning it over to Chris Watkins, an investigator with the Jackson County Medical Examiner's office. Kansas City Removal Services transported the body to the Medical Examiner's Office where Sgt. Bernard was waiting so that the identification process could be taken in an entirely new direction. Now the body of the decapitated child was examined again. It was preserved and shrunken and oily in appearance. Frank Bender had returned the skull in good condition, but the flesh depth markers used to create the original bust were still on it, in direct opposition to the standard practice for reburying human remains. Mary H. Manhein, the director of Louisiana State University's Forensic Anthropology and Computer Enhancement Services (FACES) Lab, offered to recreate the face. It would prove to be the most realistic image of the actual child. She came to KC in July 2003 to pick up the skull and take it to the FACES lab in a discreet plastic container. It looked like someone's lunch.

In August 2003, Bernard went to Baton Rouge to pick up the sculpture/skull at the FACES Lab on the campus of Louisiana State University. He took along a wooden box custom-built to the lab's specifications by KCPD building maintenance. This container was designed to allow Bernard to transport the sculpture/skull back to Kansas City safely. Mary Manhein picked up the head and carefully placed it in the container. The soft clay image lay upon Precious Doe's skull and she was frozen in time. She was trapped in a likeness that most could not identify, and the few who could remember the little girl chose to look the other way. Precious Doe sat waiting for someone to rescue her.

Sue Stiltner from VICAP contacted Sgt. Ike Vavasseur of the Baton Rouge Police Department to facilitate the transport as the skull had to be hand-carried due to the consistency of the clay. Running the sculpture through the X-ray check on the conveyor belt would have destroyed the image that had been so painstakingly constructed on the skull. The TSA staff at the airport escorted Sgt. Bernard through the metal detector and onto the plane. The burly white police sergeant was walking through the airport with a little black girl's head in the box. Knowing the box's contents, the visual must have made for some interesting discussions in the TSA breakroom. There was a seat next to Bernard purchased specifically for this trip. Precious Doe was strapped in for her first and only plane ride, and she and her protector were on their way home. The flight attendants asked what it was, and after the plane landed, he gingerly opened the box and showed them as he shared the story of Precious Doe. A couple seated near him "had to ask," so Bernard told the story of this little girl's journey so far. It seemed like a grim version of the Seńor Wences routine from the old Ed Sullivan Show when he talks to the head in the box. "Sar right?" "Sar right."

On September 14, 2003, another press conference presented this new sculpture. It gained national attention once again. *USA Today* picked up the story, and Mary Manhein was featured along with the staff from the FACES Lab. The team at FACES is a fantastic group of modern-day masters who continue to refine what Leonardo Da Vinci started centuries before—bridging art and science.

With the assistance of the FBI, a testing facility was identified to conduct specialized stable isotope analysis of Precious Doe's hair, bones, and teeth in late Fall 2004. This testing could determine if she was from the Midwest or was brought there from another part of the country or outside the United States. There is a relationship between the stable isotope ratios of food and water and the stable isotopes of humans. Therefore, the isotope ratios are analyzed in human blood, hair, bone, muscle, and teeth. When these ratios are compared to percentages in geographical areas of the United States, a possible determination can be made as to a person's origins or the area in which they live.

Along with the victim's biological samples, six sets of tissue, hair, and bone samples from recently deceased children from the Kansas City area were provided for comparison purposes. Additionally, it could determine the food and water sources specific to a particular geo-location by measuring the oxygen, carbon, hydrogen, and sulfur levels.

Simply put, based on the premise that you "are what you eat," this scientific process afforded investigators reliable forensic evidence of the victim's geographic origin and possible travel movements. At the time of Precious Doe's murder, the average DNA testing only examined 13 genetic traits. However, utilizing a private DNA lab in Florida that specialized in DNA analysis for biogeographical ancestry afforded 184 different markers to be measured.

Coupled with the DNA used to identify ethnicity through biogeographical profiling and the dental forensics and medical examiner's reports, the scientific data helped the detectives narrow down the identity of the as-yet unidentified child.

Her Name Is Erica Green

Detective Teddy Taylor took the call from Thurman McIntosh on Friday, April 29, 2005, the day after the fourth anniversary of the discovery of Precious Doe's body. The caller had seen the ad sponsored by General Mills Foods in his copy of *The Call* newspaper, a local Kansas City publication that employed a relative of McIntosh's. Taylor took down all the information and knew that it sounded good. The caller was confused and hard to understand, but the details provided a clear enough picture to see a viable lead when the dots were connected. It was the first substantial lead in months. Knowing this would require serious investigation, he told McIntosh they would call him back on Monday. In the meantime, he took the information to Sgt. Bernard and they began the weekend by running down this lead at a frenetic pace.

McIntosh provided the name Michelle Green (aka Johnson), and it came up in the database. Not only had she lived in the neighborhood, but she had also provided a statement to police on a possible suspect.

Robert D. Keppel, an internationally known homicide investigator and criminal justice professor who worked on such high-profile cases as the Ted Bundy serial murders and the Green River Murder Task Force, theorized that 95% of the time, a killer's name would appear in the first 30 days of a criminal investigation and his hypothesis was correct.

However, when Michelle Johnson was contacted at what would later be determined was the scene of the location of the crime, she provided a false description of a potential suspect seen in the area when she answered the door.

A call was placed to the Muskogee police to obtain background on a married couple named Michelle and Harrell Johnson, but they were asked only to determine if they were still in Oklahoma and not to take any action. In opposition to the Kansas City police request, the Muskogee Police, in their infinite wisdom, used the couple's outstanding traffic warrants and immediately took them into custody. Harrell commented to Michelle in front of the police that he guessed it was about "that thing in Kansas City." Directions are not followed well in Oklahoma. Maybe this is why it's called the Sooner State. They'd sooner do it their way than listen to anyone. This accelerated the travel plans for Kansas City Detectives Tammy Payne and Danny Phillips, who were sent to Muskogee, Oklahoma, on Wednesday, May 4, 2005. There was no getting this genie back in the bottle.

While all this was transpiring, McIntosh called a local activist on Saturday. He thought the police weren't working it because they said they'd call him back. He was wrong. One should never assume. He promised to send evidence that Michelle was Precious Doe's mother and that he had photos to help identify the child. He did, and the packet McIntosh sent was turned over to the police on Tuesday. It contained hair samples and pictures, one with a note indicating that he believed the little girl was Michelle's daughter, Erica Green. He sent what he believed was a photograph of the child with other family members, but it was **not** a photo of Erica Green; however, it was released to the media by the activist. The wrong little girl would end up all over the news, and her picture remains on the Internet today, associated with Precious Doe articles. During her interview with police detectives in May 2005, Michelle Johnson annotated a copy of that photograph, writing the name of each individual next to their image. The child was Michelle Johnson's niece.

The hair samples McIntosh forwarded were pubic hairs that he had fraudulently obtained from Michelle (Green) Johnson, who reluctantly agreed to provide them in exchange for $600.00 cash. During his May 1, 2005 statement to police, McIntosh bragged about how he had convinced Michelle that he needed her head and pubic hairs so he could place them in the family Bible on the page with Psalm 23, which would protect her from danger. McIntosh's intention, however, was for this to be used as DNA evidence to collect the $33,000.00 reward. He successfully collected both. In an ironic twist of fate, it was she who pulled her child off the path of righteousness and dragged her lifeless body through a proverbial valley of the shadow of death, anointing her head with the contents of a dirty garbage bag.

Psalm 23 (King James Version)

23 The Lord is my shepherd; I shall not want.

2 He maketh me to lie down in green pastures: he leadeth me beside the still waters.

3 He restoreth my soul: he leadeth me in the paths of righteousness for his name's sake.

4 Yea, though I walk through the valley of the shadow of death, I will fear no evil: for thou art with me; thy rod and thy staff they comfort me.

5 Thou preparest a table before me in the presence of mine enemies: thou anointest my head with oil; my cup runneth over.

6 Surely goodness and mercy shall follow me all the days of my life: and I will dwell in the house of the Lord forever.

In a podcast interview some years later, Michelle confirmed that she gave this hair sample to McIntosh. She said he wanted to keep them in the family Bible to remember her as she had provided sex to him and his son, her husband's uncle.

The interviews that Danny and Tammy conducted started with Michelle on May 4th. Record searches would reveal that she went by the following names: Michelle Green, Michelle Pierce, Michelle Pierece, Tonya Nudley, Michelle Marie Johnson, Michelle D Green, Michelle Marie Green, Tonya Annette Nudley, Michelle Desire Pierce, Michelle Marie Pierece, Michelle M. Green, Michelle Shaute Desha Green, Michelle M Pierce, Michelle M Johnson. She was told why they were there and was given a photo to look at for confirmation. This was an actual photo of Erica provided by her foster mother, Betty Brown, not McIntosh's erroneous photo. She identified the child in the picture as her little girl. She confirmed that the child was Erica Michelle Marie Green. She also confirmed that she knew the child was the one Kansas City residents called Precious Doe, the unidentified victim found at 59th and Kensington. She was asked if she'd like to write a note to Erica on the photograph as she signed and dated the back for detectives. She indicated that she would like to do that and wrote *"To Erica Green"* on the back of the picture. *"Moma (sic) is so sorry. You are always in my heart and soul. Love you always, 'little E.'"*

Michelle told the detectives how she was raped by her uncle and a family friend as a little girl and that she left school at 13 when she met Erica's father. She quickly began to use drugs with him and he got her into prostitution, working as her pimp. They had their first child when she was 16 years old, and by that time, he had her using crack cocaine regularly. They would have four more children before she left him when he was incarcerated. She spoke about the Illinois Department of Family Services removing three of her children from her custody and giving them to her mother and that another had been placed in a foster home and subsequently adopted. He had been extremely abusive and controlling to her, and when she met Harrell, one of her johns, they started a relationship that was only slightly better than what she had with Erica's father.

She explained to the detective how they were on the run due to Harrell's outstanding warrants in Oklahoma and that she had retrieved Erica and taken her to Kansas City to collect more welfare benefits. In one of Harrell's drugged-out rages, he kicked Erica in the head and knocked her across the room. Michelle stated that she yelled at Harrell and said, "What did you do?" She noted that Erica would not move, and she picked her up and ran her under the faucet in the bathtub but could not rouse the child. She remained unresponsive and wouldn't eat the food or swallow the water Michelle tried to give her. She rocked the comatose child and sang to her but could not get her to open her eyes or move. She could tell the little girl was still breathing, but Michelle and Harrell panicked and would not call the police because of the warrants.

Michelle tried to explain the inexplicable—she couldn't get her dying child medical attention because she had warrants for writing bad checks. Her baby is slowly dying from a traumatic brain injury, but all Michelle Johnson could do was worry about herself and her criminal boyfriend. She testified to these facts in court, giving testimony against Harrell at his trial.

Finally, the child died about 24 hours later and Harrell devised a plan to dispose of the body. Harrell climbed out the bedroom window as soon as it was nighttime and Michelle handed over her dead baby. She accompanied Harrell to the wooded area across from the church down the street and he cut off Erica's head with a pair of hedge clippers he took from the house where they lived. Next, he picked up her head, stuffed it into a trash bag, tossed it into the church's dumpster, and took the body farther into the woods. When Michelle learned about where the head was, she retrieved it from the dumpster and tossed it into the woods as she feared that someone from the church would smell the decay and find the head. She did not think about her child. No, she merely worried about getting caught. Two days earlier, she tried to revive the baby with the bath water, and now she's throwing her out with it. This action is poetic and pathetic when considering the irony it presents.

She elaborated on how she explained to her family about Erica's whereabouts when she and Harrell left Kansas City and returned to Illinois. Her excuse was that Larry Green was not Erica's father and that the child was now residing with her biological father, a school teacher in Oklahoma, who was taking excellent care of the child. However, DNA results from buccal swabs from Michelle Johnson and Larry Green would ultimately confirm that she and Green were the child's natural parents.

During the interview, she requested that she be allowed to talk to Harrell before his interrogation began. It was risky, but Sgt. Bernard approved it, and Muskogee P.D. agreed and arranged the meeting. They had Michelle's statement about her involvement in Erica's death, so the hope was that by her talking to him, he'd know she'd given them both up and that telling the truth was his best option.

It was 1:20 a.m., and the meeting was held in the sergeant's office at the Muskogee Police Department. Neither suspect was handcuffed, and they were allowed to sit on the chairs set up for them to sit directly in front of each other. Danny Phillips and three sergeants from the Muskogee Police Department were in the room with them.

Within minutes of Michelle stating that it was over and that he needed to tell the detectives what happened, Harrell began to cry. His knees touched hers when she told him he needed to tell the truth because she had already told the whole story. He said he would "just to get her out," believing if he claimed this was an accident, Michelle would not be held accountable for her significant role in this crime, hoping she would corroborate his story. However, he knew he would be charged with the Precious Doe murder when the Muskogee police took him into custody. He also knew that, when interrogated by detectives, Michelle was bound to confess, blaming him for the crime. She was no stranger to the criminal justice system and would negotiate for the best sentence possible.

Harrell had a bruise on his forehead, and when asked about it, he stated it was because he beat his head on the wall in an attempt to kill himself. He sat silent and then finally told Michelle, "it's cool. It's over with." He then began insisting it was all an accident, but she kept telling him to tell the truth. She said it would make him feel better as she had told the truth, and it was a relief of sorts to her. But he still kept insisting to her that it was an accident.

It was now 1:45 a.m., and Michelle asked if she could make a phone call. She wanted to call her mother. The detectives didn't hear the entire conversation, but they did listen to her ask her mother if she'd love her no matter what she might have done. Her mother must have answered in the affirmative because Michelle then told her that she'd lied about where Erica was and that the child had died accidentally. Oddly, this is what Harrell kept trying to convince detectives of and she knew better by her own statements. It's tragic to think that she desperately wanted to have her mother's reassurance of her love. Michelle's family was dysfunctional, and she was keenly aware of this, having been abused by her uncle and his friends. Yet, Michelle allowed her children to be placed in her parent's home—the very place where her downward spiral started at the hands of her own kin. Herbert Ward said, "Child abuse casts a shadow the length of a lifetime." Unfortunately, truer words were never spoken.

Meanwhile, the detectives took Harrell into an interview room, and he was told why they were there—to follow up on a tip regarding a murdered child in Kansas City. Harrell was read his Miranda rights from a written waiver, and he elected to waive those rights and talk to them, signing the waiver form.

Harrell was cooperative and communicative. He was given a color photo of Erica Green and acknowledged that this was his stepdaughter. When asked to initial and date the back of the picture, he did so without hesitation. Next, he began to tell the detectives that he'd been living with Michelle for three years but had actually known her longer. He was one of her johns when she worked as a prostitute in Muskogee while married to her first husband. Michelle went to prison for theft charges for two years, but she and Harrell took up again after her release and subsequent divorce from Erica's father. Harrell said he'd moved to Kansas City with her and their biological daughter in 2001. Harrell stated it was around that time that she brought Erica up to Kansas City from Muskogee, claiming the child was slightly retarded and was being abused by her foster family. He then began to tell his version of the story he referred to as "the incident" in Kansas City.

On the day Erica was murdered, Harrell drank beer and smoked a form of PCP called "wet," a cigarette dipped in the PCP. He was in the back bedroom of Rachelle Allendale's home, where he, Michelle, and the two little girls were staying. At about 9 p.m., Michelle and Erica were in the room because Michelle was trying to get the child to bed. Harrell claimed that he yelled at Erica and told her to sit down because she didn't mind her mother. She was three years old, terrified, and alone with virtual strangers, one of whom, based on forensic evidence, may have sexually assaulted her. Given that Erica was only with her mother and Harrell by their admission during these few weeks, it is not unreasonable to consider it was he who sexually assaulted the child. This could explain why she exhibited the classic behavioral signs of sexual abuse, such as shrinking away from her or seeming threatened by physical contact.

Harrell said he pushed her down to the floor with his left leg because he was "not in his right heart and mind," Erica wasn't listening, so he pushed her hard to the ground with his left leg. He also stated that he grabbed her by the shoulder and violently pushed her down, knocking her unconscious. He and Michelle then panicked when the child remained unresponsive. He told how Michelle went to get Erica a glass of water while he picked the child up and laid her on the bed. He said he thought Erica was "doing fine," but she did not speak or look at anything even though her eyes were open. Harrell then began to say that the child appeared to be in shock. He claimed that he thought her reaction resulted from prior physical abuse from her foster family and not a physical injury. The little girl lay dying, and nothing was done to try and save her. In Harrell's statement, he says it was half a day.

In Michelle's statement to the police, it is recorded as two days that the child lay dying—no one knows who is correct. It is known that there was no evidence of abuse before leaving the care of Mrs. Brown in Oklahoma, nor was she mentally challenged. Still, she was in dire need of medical attention, which she never received because of Harrell and Michelle's ignorance and calculated withholding of care. He told officers he was frantic about her death and didn't know what to do. He threatened to kill himself but couldn't muster the courage to take his own life. To keep his evil deed under wraps, he proceeded to take hedge clippers and do something even more gruesome with no apparent fear or remorse. He couldn't commit suicide, but he could mutilate an innocent little girl's lifeless body. His level of panic was overshadowed by his intent to cover his misdeeds. In the end, he valued his own life but not the life of an innocent child.

Harrell waited until the cover of night and sneaked out the bedroom window to dispose of the dead child. Michelle handed Erica's limp body to Harrell, climbed out the same window, and followed him into the wooded area down the street, across from a church parking lot. He carried Erica as though she was sleeping; Michelle following behind with a pair of hedge clippers in tow. They walked down the road into the woods and Harrell laid Erica on the ground so that Michelle could undress the little girl, leaving her naked in the dirt. Without hesitation, Harrell took the clippers and cut off the child's head with one stroke. He and Michelle then proceeded to drag the child farther into the woods. Michelle found a bag among the trash nearby, holding it as Harrell dropped Erica's head into it. He tied up the bag, took it over to the dumpster in the church parking lot, and tossed it in. Michelle didn't want to leave the head there as she feared the smell would alert someone at the church, so she retrieved it from the dumpster. Harrell then took the bag and tossed it back into the woods, away from where Erica's body was dumped. They then walked back to the house, climbed through the bedroom window, and continued their lives. He didn't know what happened to the hedge clippers.

Harrell was shown a photograph of Erica and positively identified Erica Green. He was asked to initial the back of the photo, and he wrote a note to Erica that said he was sorry for what he did. It read, *"I'm so sorry that this happened, and I hope that you forgive me for what I have done, and I will always love you with all my heart and soul. I will always miss you. Harrell Johnson, Sr."* It was small comfort for killing her and disfiguring her body. He then positively identified Michelle Johnson from another photo, dating and initialing it on the back, as requested by the detectives.

After the statements were videotaped, Michelle and Harrell were allowed briefly to meet again in the interrogation room. Monitored by video surveillance, the couple spoke while Michelle fixed Harrell's hair, pulling it back and securing it with a rubber band. She asked him what he told the police and he said he had admitted what had happened to Erica. They compared stories, and they were apparently out of step and covering for themselves and not each other on specific points. For example, Harrell had told the officers that Michelle was present when he cut Erica's head off and how she retrieved it from the dumpster.

On the other hand, Michelle said that she had gone back to the house and was not a participant in the gruesome disposition of her daughter's body. It was now after 3:00 a.m.; the jailers were standing by to escort the Johnsons to their temporary—and separate—quarters in the Muskogee County Jail. After that, they would never spend time alone together again. Due to the horrific nature of the crimes specified in the arrest warrants, Harrell was held without bond, and Michelle's bond had been set at $500,000, cash only. Neither would be going anywhere until Kansas City detectives were ready to escort them back to stand trial for the murder of the child no longer known only as Precious Doe.

Danny Phillips called David from Muskogee and said, "This is her," and asked for more help. So Sgt. Bernard and two detectives went to Oklahoma to help. Frank Booth and crime scene investigators brought the crime scene van for property recovery. Dirk Tarpley also accompanied them on behalf of the FBI.

On the trip to Muskogee, Sgt. Bernard discovered that every word of the Johnson confessions had been shared with the local paper. A Muskogee detective tried to record the confessions surreptitiously and supplied reporters with the details. Because of the information leak, Dirk arranged for the investigative team to access the FBI headquarters in Muskogee and the whole operation was moved there. A command center was established, and the Muskogee police were furious. They ripped into Det. Tammy Payne, arguing how unprofessional the Kansas City detectives were for doing this. This was an instance of the pot calling the kettle black! But at least they were prevented from harming the case and had little further involvement until the extradition process was completed. Unfortunately, the KCPD's communications group's media support would not prove much better.

The media officer who accompanied Sgt. Bernard to Muskogee was exceptionally helpful. However, the primary press conference was held in Kansas City, and the media representative who stayed behind for "the big announcement" said that the Homicide squad could have done more to solve the case sooner. The sergeant was livid. He went ballistic when he heard what his department was saying. But, for the love of God, what else could he or anyone else have humanly done when those who could have come forward failed to do so? How much harder could they have worked?

It was unfortunate that the media officer spoke before he thought. He didn't bother to consider the overarching issues before opening his mouth. It didn't bode well for the KCPD or its reputation in the community, and it certainly didn't gain the undying gratitude of the 1020 Squad. It was not the KCPD's finest hour. Perhaps he felt compelled to editorialize to keep the cameras rolling a little longer. Still, his fifteen minutes of fame expired silently and with no apparent notice, like a quarter's worth of time in a parking meter.

What the Mama Knew

During the investigation in Oklahoma, detectives were given information that Harrell had confessed about Erica's murder not only to his grandfather, Thurman McIntosh, but that Harrell's mother also knew the whole story of what happened to the child. Because of these additional witnesses, the Kansas City detectives and two sergeants from the Muskogee P.D. went to Debra Johnson's apartment to interview Debra and her father, Thurman McIntosh.

Debra Johnson was willing to go to the Muskogee police station to be interviewed, but only if her husband could drive her. Over the pizza and soda the detectives provided, Debra cordially answered questions about her basic personal information (birthdate, address, phone numbers, etc.).

The purpose of these interviews was to confirm what Harrell allegedly told his grandfather and verify that Debra Johnson had known of Erica's murder months, possibly years, before. The discussions with detectives started as a general information-gathering session to obtain details such as full name, date of birth, etc. Then they talked about her family and her interest in childcare. Finally, she spoke at length about her children and grandchildren. Debra said Harrell and Michele's three young children were all in the custody of the State of Oklahoma.

When one of the detectives elaborated on why they wanted to interview Debra, she denied knowing anything about Erica Green, her step-granddaughter, being the dead child in Kansas City known as "Precious Doe." She protested that she didn't know who Precious Doe was or what they talked about concerning the child's death. After talking over sodas and pizza for another half hour, Debra started to cry. She said she should have done something to help Erica because she knew what was going on with the drug use, the abuse, and the dysfunctional lives that Harrell and Michelle led. Debra stated she knew her son killed Erica while he lived in Kansas City. She said she was upset because she might have helped Erica and tried to save her.

Debra proceeded to tell detectives the story as she knew it. When Harrell first introduced Debra to his then-girlfriend Michelle, she used the last name Pierce and worked at fast-food restaurants. Erica had been born while Michelle was in prison, and the baby was given to Betty Brown, a foster mother in Muskogee, soon after she was born. Debra said she was aware of Erica staying with Betty Brown in Muskogee and that the last time she saw Erica was just before Michelle and Harrell's son was born. She described the couple's pattern of behavior as erratic, moving back and forth between Muskogee and Chicago every few months. She did recall them taking the bus to Kansas City in 2001 and that Michelle took Erica and her other daughter with them. She said she believed Erica's biological father was from Kansas City but thought he was in prison in Oklahoma. She couldn't remember who they stayed with, but she knew they had been in Kansas City for two or three weeks before "it happened," her reference to Erica's murder. It was learned that the Johnsons didn't go to Kansas City to reunite with family members, as Michelle had told Betty Brown. Harrell was wanted for assault and battery in Muskogee, so they were on the run from the law with no intention of returning to Oklahoma soon.

She stated that immediately after "the incident" occurred, Harrell obtained bus tickets to Chicago from a

Kansas City charity. He and Michelle took the baby to stay with Michelle's family in Chicago. When they wore out their welcome in Chicago, they asked Debra to send them bus tickets to return to Muskogee. Sometime after that, Debra sent bus tickets to the couple so they could go back to Muskogee, but she was unsure when that was.

When the couple returned to Muskogee, Michelle told Debra that Erica was with Michelle's mother in Chicago. She said she never heard Michelle call Erica "Precious Doe," but every time she saw an article about the missing child in Kansas City, Michelle would cry and say that she reminded her of her own daughter. Debra noted that this occurred before Michelle told her about what happened to Erica but that she had suspicions. Debra just never followed up on them. If she didn't ask, she wouldn't have to deal with what she might learn. The Precious Doe case had been featured on *America's Most Wanted* three times, on *MSNBC*, *The Today Show*, and *Cold Case Files*. It was in national papers, including People Magazine, USA Today, and Newsweek, and was broadcast on national news outlets. With all the notoriety, perhaps she might have put the pieces together and reported this to authorities. But then, she'd have had to face up to who she had for a son. Who knows? Maybe he took after his father.

Debra told detectives that on April 1, 2002, Michelle Green and Harrell Johnson tied the knot almost one year after their unholy union resulted in the violent death of Michelle's daughter. They were at the courthouse in Muskogee that day for Harrell's appearance on two assault charges: one for hitting someone in the head with a brick and the other for shooting someone else. The victims were "no-shows," and the judge dismissed the felony charges for shooting with intent to kill and assault and battery with a dangerous weapon. Nevertheless, Michelle and Harrell took advantage of their visit, went to another courtroom, and got married. Why waste bus fare when you can accomplish so much in a single visit to the Muskogee County Courthouse? It appeared Harrell was a practical fellow, mainly because he was living partially off welfare benefits for a child he murdered the previous year, or possibly just another hopeless romantic caught up in the giddy excitement of beating a stint in jail.

Finally, Debra Johnson disclosed that Michelle had told her what had happened with Erica Green approximately a year ago (2003 or 2004). Debra said she initially couldn't believe that her son would have killed Erica. When she learned about this, Harrell was jailed in Oklahoma on unrelated charges, but she did not attempt to contact him to confirm or dispel Michelle's accusations. Debra didn't press Michelle for any information at the time because she didn't want to think about the murder of the child. A few weeks later, however, she approached Michelle and asked for the details of what happened, and Michelle told her the whole story. Harrell's mother said Michelle expressed concern about how he would act when he got out of jail. According to Debra, Michelle couldn't have been too concerned because she stayed in town and was dating Harrell's cousin. When Harrell was finally released, he and Michelle did get back together and had another child. There is no honor among thieves or murderers, and Erica's blood wasn't thicker than the vile glue that held Michelle and Harrell together.

Debra identified Erica, Erica's biological father Larry Green, Michelle, and Harrell Johnson from photos officers showed her. She knew them all, and she knew much more. She knew what happened to Erica Green for more days, months, and years than she should have without offering anyone a single bit of that critical information. The cries of one innocent child were stifled by the very people who might have helped her or at least brought some long-overdue justice to the case.

The silence kept by so many individuals who knew Erica Green was reprehensible. Her life had been ended, but the child still needed a voice—someone to speak up on her behalf, and the very people who should have helped her kept brutally silent instead. They all talked a great deal, but the language didn't include words that spoke about Erica, let alone for her. Instead, lots of cruel, salty language was directed at the detectives during the years she went without a name. The four-letter words that needed to be said about this case—love, hope, care, help, need, safe, and most importantly, her real name—was not a part of her own family's vocabulary.

Never Put Anything in Writing

In roughly April 2005, Michelle asked Debra to destroy letters that she and Harrell had exchanged while he was in prison in Muskogee for unrelated charges. The letters were supposed to be in the car's trunk owned by Debra's father, Thurman McIntosh.

Debra retrieved the letters and put them in a trash bag, storing them in a closet in Thurman's apartment so that Michelle would not find them. Debra claimed she didn't read the letters but decided that if they were important enough that Michelle kept them, she wouldn't throw them out.

Accompanied by Muskogee officers on the afternoon of May 4, 2005, the detectives brought a search warrant. They followed up on Debra Johnson's information that her father (Thurman McIntosh) had letters that Harrell had written to Michelle and kept those in the trunk of his 1991 silver Oldsmobile Cutlass. She further stated that some letters and documents were in a trash bag she had stored in his apartment. McIntosh agreed to the searches, but when detectives looked in the vehicle, it was full of trash and junk, and no letters were found. The results of the apartment visit would prove to be more productive.

Just inside the apartment was a closet filled with bags and other items. On the closet floor, detectives located a white trash bag that held the letters Debra had referenced. Michelle's black duffle bag was also found there. It contained more letters from Harrell, a cell phone, an address book, and a make-up bag that stored Social Security cards for Michelle Johnson and Erica Green. Ironically, a birth announcement for Erica Green from the University of Oklahoma Hospital was also found. She threw away the baby but kept the announcement. The insanity had no bounds.

Some of the letters that the police retrieved from Thurman McIntosh's apartment could best be described as revolting. Harrell's concerns were for cigarettes and sex, encouraging Michelle to get a driver's license, stay off drugs, and get a job so that when he was released from prison, he could be a stay-at-home dad, like one he'd recently seen on the prison television. He wrote about "little E," as Erica was called, sometimes apologetically and sometimes threatening Michelle with going to the police if she didn't comply with whatever he was ranting about on any particular day. His descriptions of what he was doing in the shower at the prison and what he planned to do with Michelle when he returned were deviant and disgusting. His idea of romance left little to the imagination and proffered a mental picture that scarred the mind and numbed the senses.

Harrell's threats about Erica didn't sit well with Michelle. She wrote to Harrell that she was loyal to him, an excellent mother to their children (including the one she was pregnant with), and that he should never have used the issue with Erica to threaten her. She threatened to break off the relationship, but unfortunately, later correspondence and history showed that their love was here to stay.

The TIPS Hotline Caller

When the detectives arrived at the apartment, McIntosh appeared glad to see the officers and tell the story of what he believed happened to the child he referred to as his great-granddaughter. He took the detectives to his vehicle, where they recovered a photo McIntosh wanted them to have, stating that it was a photo of Michelle Johnson and her children. It was a copy of the image he said he mailed to *The Call* newspaper in Kansas City. However, he remained cooperative and agreed to go to the police station for his formal interview.

At the police station, McIntosh related that his stepdaughter worked for *The Call* newspaper in Kansas City and that he had a subscription, and that's where he saw the ad for information about the murdered child in Kansas City. As the story unfolded, McIntosh detailed the relationship between Michelle and Harrell, their jailhouse marriage in Oklahoma (after Erica was murdered), and how he thought Michelle had five children from prior relationships, one named Erica Green. The older man believed he had seen the little girl once but wasn't sure about it. However, he did know the names of the children Michelle had with Harrell, the one they had with them when Erica was alive, and the two born during the years after Erica's death. Throughout the investigation, rumors surfaced that dear old "grandpa" had more than a slight interest in Harrell's wife. Still, the allegations of a relationship between them were not substantiated until the detectives interviewed Thurman McIntosh in Oklahoma. Years later, during a podcast interview, Michelle admitted having sex with both McIntosh and his son, Harrell's uncle.

The ad Thurman McIntosh had seen in the publication was placed and funded by the General Mills Company. It ran in the April 22 – 28th edition of a Kansas City newspaper and was written by the General Mills Vice President of Communications. It was a half-page with a photo of the sketch of Precious Doe and a headline that read, "We will not forget."

A local activist claimed credit for supposedly writing and paying for the ad, but General Mills confirmed that their organization ran them at his insistence. He also claimed credit for singlehandedly solving the case. But unfortunately, McIntosh didn't call him first—he called a day after he called the police, who were aggressively following this new lead, documenting their findings, and actively trying to keep the information out of the media.

A Genuine Love

It was May 6, 2005, and the detectives headed out early in the morning to Betty Brown's residence to speak with her daughters: Nancy Jackson and Dorothy Webster. Mrs. Brown was contacted, but her daughters were not there. However, she did indicate that she could give a statement and get the detectives in contact with her daughters by phone. They contacted Dorothy Webster, who willingly agreed to meet the detectives at Mrs. Brown's house. Mrs. Brown's cooperative nature was evidenced even in the face of the subject she was about to discuss. Her losing Erica was a devastating experience, especially when the news was still such a fresh and gaping wound.

She told the detectives the story of her years as a foster mother and how she met Michelle Johnson through Michelle's then mother-in-law, the mother of Erica's biological father. She recalled the phone call she received from a pregnant Michelle, who was incarcerated in the Mabel Bassett Correctional Center in Oklahoma City right before her baby was to be born. Michelle needed someone to take custody of the baby because she still had three more months to serve her sentence. So Mrs. Green got the child protective services agency approval to foster a baby named Erica Michelle Marie Green, who would be born on May 15, 1997. The baby was delivered at a hospital in Oklahoma City, and Mrs. Brown picked her up the day she was born.

The plan was that she would remain with Mrs. Brown until her mother was released from jail.

Michelle was released when Erica was about three months old but didn't retrieve her baby. The infant remained with Mrs. Brown, and Michelle only came to visit two or three times a year. Erica was Betty Brown's child for all intents and purposes, spending her days with Mrs. Brown and going home with Brown's daughter, Dorothy, at night.

In the first week of April 2001, Michelle concocted a story about a family reunion in Oklahoma City and convinced Mrs. Brown that Erica should go with her. By law, the foster mother had to defer to Michelle. It was only for the weekend and seemed to be just another of Michelle's once-in-a-blue-moon attempts to be a mother to Erica. But the blue moon turned night into day, and the days began to pass. The day would never come when Mrs. Brown would see Erica again. Not in this lifetime.

Mrs. Brown did hear from Michelle during the last week of April. Michelle was in Kansas City and wanted Mrs. Brown to send her $50 to bring Erica back to Muskogee. Thinking that this was just another of Michelle's ploys to get money, she told Michelle she'd give her the money when she and Erica arrived back in Oklahoma. They never came.

Michelle eventually returned to Oklahoma, and she and Mrs. Brown crossed paths three different times, and each time, Michelle would give some trumped-up story about where Erica was and with whom. Once Michelle was employed as a Salvation Army bell ringer, a position that only required a government-issued identification and a Social Security card at that time. She was at a grocery store and, in the spirit of the season, claimed Erica was living happily ever after with her aunt in Kansas City. It gives one pause to think that her child would never see another Christmas. Yet, she could cavalierly brag that the child was alive and well in a city where the residents desperately wondered about the unknown little victim found two years ago.

The next time she ran into Mrs. Brown, Michelle claimed the child was off visiting "granny" in Chicago. The final time was in January 2005 when Michelle worked at McDonald's inside the Muskogee Wal-Mart. Michelle insisted that Erica was fine and left it at that. That was Michelle—serving up fries and lies and not missing a beat. Mrs. Brown was such a lovely and gentle woman. Until the Kansas City detectives contacted her, she had no idea that Erica was deceased.

She didn't have anything else she could share with the officers except that she loved Erica. This poor lady suffered so much over the untimely loss of this little girl that she considered her own child. This was devastating for her, and as she concluded her comments, the officers began to interview Dorothy Webster, who had arrived just as she had promised.

The Baby on the Bus Says, "Wah, wah, wah!"

Dorothy Webster remembered so many happy things about Erica's life. She told about how her mother raised Erica and how she would visit Betty after work almost daily and help care for Erica. Dorothy remarked how attached she was to Erica, playing with her and teaching her to spell her name and how she could sing her favorite song, "The Wheels on the Bus." She said that Erica had a good vocabulary and spoke clearly for her age. She bought Erica clothes and said she liked dressing up for church, wearing hats, and carrying purses. Erica loved the church activities and had a loving upbringing in the care of her foster family. She loved to watch *Tele-Tubbies* and *Barney and Friends*. Dorothy bragged that Erica was potty trained and could bathe herself. Her favorite toy was a pillow that played the song "Good Night, Good Night" when she squeezed it. She described Erica as a real child, not the nameless victim in a case file. It was bittersweet.

Her mood darkened when asked about Erica's birth mother. Dorothy said she knew Michelle but never met Harrell Johnson. She described how Michelle would blow in and out of Erica's life, taking her for a little while and then bringing her back to Mrs. Brown when she was "through fooling with her," as she put it. She stated it was easy to tell when Erica had gone with her mother. Dorothy noted that the child was visibly not well cared for, although she was never bruised or appeared to have been hit or mistreated. She was just an afterthought in Michelle's world. She remarked how Michelle never asked about Erica's allergies. When the detectives inquired what she meant, she described how Erica would break out in a rash from mosquito bites and had the same reaction if given Motrin or any other over-the-counter ibuprofen product.

The detectives asked Dorothy if Erica was called by any other names, and Dorothy commented that Erica was called "Little E." Dorothy remarked that the last time Michelle came to take Erica to what was supposed to be a family reunion, she never saw Erica again.

Later in the afternoon, detectives and crime scene investigators returned to Mrs. Brown's house with the warrant for the search of her property. She had agreed to this during her interview. They took the obligatory photographs and some items Mrs. Brown identified as Erica's. The ever-increasing evidence began forming a case against Harrell and Michelle Johnson. God willing, it would be enough.

During the interview, Dorothy recalled that she might have some items of Erica's in a storage locker, so a warrant was obtained for that location, and the detectives and CSI crew headed out again. Dorothy couldn't locate her key to the storage locker, so personnel from the storage facility were contacted, but they didn't have a duplicate key. The renter of the locker provides the lock and key. The Muskogee Fire Department had to be contacted to respond and cut the lock. Every time the detectives got a little closer to Erica, some supernatural roadblock was conjured up to slow the process down again. The powers of good and evil? Who knows, but whatever it was, it was a frustration that didn't seem to have an end. The locker was finally searched and some clothing and toys of Erica's were recovered. Mrs. Brown had maintained the belongings of each of her foster children in an organized fashion. She meticulously gathered all of Erica's personal items—right down to her hairbrush—and placed them in storage. Among the things recovered by detectives was a stuffed "Big Bird," a baby doll, and a toy telephone. The life of Erica Michelle Marie Green in Oklahoma was taking shape as well, and it was a far different image than that of the little mutilated child who had lain alone and unloved in a dump in Kansas City.

59th and Kensington

While the interviews with Erica's foster family were occurring, detectives back in Kansas City tracked down the new resident of the house where Erica had died. They located the woman at work and learned that she lived there with her three children but had only stayed at the residence for a few months. Until the detectives talked to her, the occupant was unaware of the gruesome history of her new home. Finally, she agreed to let the police into her house and willingly signed the consent-to-search form, providing keys to the residence while still trying to comprehend the information she had just learned. Crime Scene Technician (CST) Charlie Closson processed the home's interior while CST Lori Keller sketched the floor plan.

There was nothing special about the house on 59th Street. It was a nondescript little bungalow that sat high on a terrace with a cluttered, dirty basement and overgrown yard. The search didn't reveal anything helpful to the case, and the pair of hedge clippers used to decapitate Erica was nowhere to be found. This was formerly a little middle-class residential area, but the original families left decades earlier. So now the structure was just another rental house in a neighborhood rife with trash and long-neglected properties.

When the detectives returned the keys to the resident, she said she was planning to move soon. She didn't indicate if the news of what transpired in the house had anything to do with it. Late that evening, she left one of the detectives a voice message and indicated that she was upset by all the media attention besieging her and her neighborhood. She was another innocent victim of the horrific crime that had occurred in that house.

The Merry Month of May

During the first week of May 2005, interviews continued in Muskogee, Oklahoma, with more of Michelle and Harrell's family and friends. Detective Steve Miller and Special Agent Dirk Tarpley interviewed Lamont Allendale at the FBI office. Allendale was the brother of Rachelle Allendale and was living with her when Harrell and Michelle Johnson moved into her house on 59th Street in Kansas City. He stated that he had to give up his room in the back of the house so the Johnsons and their two children could reside there because they were paying Rachelle Allendale for the space. He indicated that he stayed with various family members while the paying customers used his room. As far as Rachelle Allendale was concerned, blood wasn't thicker than the cash and food stamps she was collecting from her new tenants.

Allendale told the police that he was aware that the older child was a two or three-year-old named Erica but didn't know the name or age of the younger child. All he was sure of was that this was Michelle's child from another relationship before her involvement with Harrell. He said this was the first time he had met Michelle and the children, but he knew Harrell because they were distantly related, but he wasn't sure of the exact connection.

He did elaborate on what he knew about the relationship between Erica, her mother, and Harrell. He said Harrell yelled at Erica and made her cry, but he never saw him hit the child. He claimed that Rachelle Allendale told him that Harrell would beat Erica with a wire hanger, and once he beat her so severely, Rachelle Allendale went and told Michelle to make him stop. This failure to act begs the question, whatever happened to someone stepping up and doing the right thing? Didn't she have the moral courage to protect that child? It's one thing to not interfere with parental discipline. It's another to allow a child to be severely beaten by someone like Harrell Johnson. Rachelle Allendale would ultimately kick the Johnsons out of the house after Harrell stole items from her home. Harrell took "charity begins at home" a little too seriously for her liking.

A Silence That Spoke Volumes

The shotgun scatter that was the 1020 squad continued on the streets of Muskogee, spreading already scarce resources even thinner. Then, while in the police station pulling earlier information together, detectives received a phone call from Rachelle Allendale.

She stated that Michelle and Harrell Johnson rented a room in her home on 59th Street in Kansas City, Missouri, during the early months of 2001, near the park where Precious Doe's body was found at approximately the same time.

Rachelle said she traveled to Muskogee with Michelle to pick up Michelle's little girl but couldn't remember the child's name. She recalled that Harrell appeared to hate the child and beat her severely, making the child vomit. These details would explain the marks the medical examiner found on the child's back, corroborating the beatings and wire hanger explanations that would surface during the case. She referred to her as "the baby" and said she was kept in the back room the Johnsons rented, was seldom let out, and was never allowed to play with Rachelle's children. When the little girl cried, Harrell would say, "You better go get that mother-fucker before I do something!" indicating Michelle should deal with "the baby." She noted that there were times when "the baby" would not eat. The child was terrified and lost in a world so foreign to her.

Rachelle described how Harrell (who she called Pete) had such violent behavior that he beat Michelle almost daily and damaged the walls in the home. Michelle picked up a knife and tried to stab Harrell during one particularly violent argument. Because the fighting escalated, Rachelle finally had to "put them out," It was then that she noticed that "the baby" seemed to be missing. When they were asked to leave, Michelle told her they would stay in Chicago with her family. According to Rachelle, this transpired when a child's body was found in the woods near her home.

She said Michelle called her from Chicago about two weeks after "Precious Doe's" body was found and that she asked Michelle about "the baby." She indicated that both her daughters were with her in Chicago. Rachelle's statements were inconsistent, and her recollections were challenging to follow. Nevertheless, she bounced back and forth with Harrell and Michelle Johnson through the events.

Rachelle said that after the violent fight with her husband, Michelle said she was taking the children and going to a battered women's shelter, but Michelle returned the following day and packed up her things. "The little girl" was not with her. Michelle left again and didn't return until early evening. She was "bloody" and breathless, sweating as though she'd been running. Harrell was nowhere around.

Rachelle gave conflicting times and information, bouncing from one topic to another. She related that around 7:00 p.m. on the same day Michelle left, Kansas City police officers came to her door looking for Harrell because of "what he had done." She said that Harrell had "jumped" bail because he had an outstanding warrant for attempted murder with a bond of $50,000.00. Supposedly Michelle told her that before she and Harrell moved to Kansas City, he had cut some lady's finger off and pawned her diamond ring. She said that's all she knew about it. With his history of violence, removing a child's head before he disposed of her seemed the logical next step in escalating violence.

Apparently, the detectives figured it wasn't worth asking if he removed the finger before he pawned the ring.

She then started to change her story and said that it was around 11:30 p.m. on the same day that Michelle returned to her house with blood on herself. According to Rachelle, Michelle mentioned that Harrell gave her a bloody nose, but she didn't see anything wrong with Michelle's face to indicate that she had been hit. When asked for more detail, Rachelle changed her story once again. She said it was closer to 10:00 p.m. when she was outside her residence on the front porch with her neighbor and "play cousin" and their children.

While they were all outside, she heard a scream from down the street in the wooded area where "Precious Doe's" body was later found. She believed the cry sounded like Michelle's "little girl's" voice that she heard. She said that when this occurred, she noticed a white station wagon with brown wood-like siding parked down the street facing the wrong direction on the road. She said she got scared and made everyone go into her house. But unfortunately, that was all she remembered. She was asked if she'd be willing to talk to officers further about this at a later date and she agreed.

The Skeleton in the Landlady's Closet

On May 6, 2005, officers went to Rachelle Allendale's apartment, where they contacted her and her mother, Naomi Allendale. They were asked if they would be willing to go with the officers to the FBI office and give another interview with the officers as part of the investigation. They agreed to do so.

Naomi Allendale began by telling officers how she came to reside in Oklahoma after being laid off from her job in Kansas City in 2004. Before that move, she had lived most of her life in Missouri. She said that Michelle Johnson had returned to Oklahoma by then. Harrell had initially been from Oklahoma, so it was no surprise that the couple had returned there. However, Harrell, or Pete as he was known to his family, was now a guest of the prison system. Michelle was again homeless, having been kicked out of her apartment complex. Harrell was family because his mother and Naomi's late husband were first cousins. This was how they knew Rachelle Allendale and came to rent a room from her in Kansas City in 2001.

She was asked if she could recall the events when the body was discovered near her daughter, Rachelle Allendale's house in Kansas City. Naomi said she stayed on 59th street with Rachelle Allendale until she could get a job and then moved out. This was about the same time Harrell and Michelle moved into the back room at Rachelle Allendale's, bringing their baby daughter. Several weeks later, Michelle and Rachelle Allendale hopped a bus for Oklahoma (courtesy of a local charity's emergency fund) to pick up one of Michelle's children from her first marriage. Naomi indicated that this was Erica Green, Michelle's only child in foster care. Michelle's other children were in her mother's custody in Illinois. They returned to Kansas City with Erica, and it was only a few weeks later that the story of Precious Doe hit the papers.

Naomi stated that Harrell was nowhere around shortly after the body was discovered. Michelle took the baby and left Rachelle Allendale's home, saying she'd sent Erica to live with her other kids in Chicago. Michelle would call and allude to the fact that she was out of town, but she and Harrell stayed in the area for a few more weeks.

Naomi said that Rachelle Allendale's boyfriend lived with her while the Johnsons stayed at the house on 59th along with Rachelle Allendale's five young daughters. She indicated that Michelle didn't work and thought Harrell spent his time burglarizing homes in the area when he wasn't doing drugs. It was crowded and chaotic, with three additional people living in the back bedroom. Then Michelle added a fourth person when she retrieved Erica from Oklahoma. She brought her back to collect assistance in Missouri for Erica since Michelle didn't have access to the welfare Mrs. Brown received in Oklahoma for Erica's benefit. She wasn't a child to the Johnsons—she was a profit center.

Erica spent her days just sitting on the sofa and was usually crying. She was never allowed outside and didn't play with Rachelle Allendale's daughters. She was just a frightened little girl who had been abducted from the safety of her home and might as well have been a hostage in a foreign land. Nothing was familiar to her. Because she cried, Harrell would scream at her, take her into the back room, and beat her. Naomi indicated that she didn't know what means were used to abuse the child, but that she'd cry hard and then she'd quiet down and whimper. She never saw her come out of the room after the beatings, so she had no recollection of the child's physical condition. Michelle would also whip the child. Neither of the Allendales ever intervened on the little girl's behalf. They were just more bystanders to a crime that should never have happened, leaving the small child to remain a hostage to fate.

During her visits to the home, which she said were three or four times a week, Naomi never saw anyone feed Erica or hold her. Instead, the little girl sat hopelessly alone in a room devoid of toys or hope. She was never allowed to play and only got beaten. It must have been a family tradition because Naomi said that Harrell abused Michelle and she often had black eyes and bruises. They fought constantly, and the drug use they both participated in only made it worse. Naomi stated she was aware of them smoking marijuana and crack cocaine.

The couple dropped out of sight for about a year after leaving Rachelle Allendale's but then showed up on Naomi's doorstep asking to stay with her, with a new baby in tow. When Naomi inquired about the whereabouts of the two other children that previously stayed with them at Rachelle Allendale's, Michelle claimed they were in Chicago with her mother. It seemed to be a reasonable response since the couple had been staying in Chicago before their return to Kansas City. However, no one thought to question them further.

The couple stayed with Naomi for two weeks, and then she had to ask them to leave. Their constant fighting was disruptive and Harrell fought with Naomi's son, who also lived with her. To make matters worse, Naomi's boyfriend resided in the home and required significant medical care as he recovered from a severe accident. Finally, Naomi's stress proved too much, so she decided that the Johnsons and their baby had to go. Detectives asked where the other two gentlemen were now, and Naomi indicated that her son was in prison in Hutchinson, Kansas. Her boyfriend had since passed away from his injuries.

Naomi was asked about the relationship between her son and Harrell and if she remembered an incident involving a gun or camera. She said she thought it was over Harrell's black semi-automatic handgun and that he had accused her son of stealing it.

She wasn't asked why she didn't speak up when Erica was beaten or if she even interacted kindly with the tragic little soul who seemed so unhappy and alone. Indifference seemed to be hereditary in this family. She never volunteered any information if she suspected the body in the woods might have been the little girl who stayed at Rachelle Allendale's those few weeks in April 2001. At this juncture, it seemed inconsequential. There isn't a law against apathy.

Accomplice in a Lie

Rachelle Allendale was interviewed again, and this time around she noted that she and Harrell are first cousins. She met Michelle about a year before she and Harrell moved into her house on 59th St. As best she could recall, this was in 2001. Before that, Michelle, Harrell, and their baby would stay with Rachelle's mom, Naomi Allendale, at her address on College Avenue. Then, they'd come and go, remaining only a few days or weeks, subjecting the child to a life of instability and dysfunction.

There should be a law against people like Rachelle Allendale, but unfortunately, apathy isn't illegal. There was a crime she was guilty of, although she was never charged. It's called welfare fraud because she took over $200 in food stamps and $300 in welfare benefits from Michelle and Harrell. The idea of renting out her back bedroom to them was her brother Waylon's, but she agreed. The Johnsons brought their baby daughter when they first arrived, and Erica would come some weeks later. Food stamps are the gold standard for barter for liquor, drugs, or even sex in "the 'hood." Perhaps getting a job and cashing a paycheck would have been too taxing on either of the Johnsons, and it was easier for Michelle to retrieve Erica from the safety of her foster home and use her as a raise in "pay." State records show that she was collecting Aid to Dependent Children for Erica in three different jurisdictions, applying for Illinois benefits after the child was deceased. She had the requisite birth certificate and no one asked to see the little girl.

During this version of events, Rachelle claimed that the last time she saw Michelle and her two little girls was before noon one day in the Spring of 2001. As she recalled, Michelle had left with the little girls but returned early in the evening with blood on her shirt. She said the baby was in the car outside with an unknown man who gave them a ride. Although the child was alone in a car with a stranger, Rachelle didn't bother to look out the window. Her only concern with Erica was that she was eligible for food stamps. She claimed that Michelle told her that Mrs. Brown had come and taken Erica back to Muskogee and that Harrell was with his uncle, who also lived in Kansas City. Michelle insisted she was taking the other baby and heading back to Chicago on the 10:00 p.m. bus. The source of Rachelle's extra income was departing on the northbound Greyhound.

As her story continued, Ms. Rachelle Allendale's recollection of events suddenly veered off course again. This version had the honorable Rachelle Allendale throwing the Johnsons out after they had a physical brawl in her home. They fought in front of the children, which was apparently the last straw for her. She claimed that this was the last time she dealt with Harrell. Michelle was packing up and planning to take the girls to a local battered women's shelter. She said that Michelle came back the following day, toting the girls in a stroller—Erica appeared to be asleep with her hands crossed on her chest. She said Michelle then left again. Michelle offered no plausible explanation for the sudden reappearance of the child she previously insisted was in Oklahoma with her foster mother.

Rachelle stated Michelle left the house again with the children and didn't return until early evening, with blood on her shirt. This was consistent with what she said previously—the same song, second verse. This time, however, Rachelle recalled asking Michelle what had happened. She got the response that Harrell hit her and gave her a bloody nose, although Rachelle recounted that Michelle's face seemed to look okay. She told Michelle to clean up, and she did. She said Michelle also packed some bags and left the house, but she didn't offer any speculation as to where the girls were while this all transpired.

As detectives attempted to clarify discrepancies in her statements, Rachelle bounced back and forth with her information. For example, after Michelle cleaned off the blood, she said Michelle sat on the couch and made a phone call to someone. She believed Michelle called Mrs. Brown to arrange for her to pick up Erica. After the call, Michelle grabbed her bags and left. Later, Rachelle Allendale would recant that portion of her story and revert to verse one, "Michelle left in a car with a stranger….".

Suddenly the story took a sharp turn as Rachelle's train of thought started to derail. She began talking about a barbeque that her mother, Naomi, and Naomi's boyfriend held a few weeks after Rachelle allegedly threw the Johnsons out of her house. Her brothers and their families were in attendance, and so was Harrell, who was brandishing a handgun. She described it as a handgun, a .32 revolver, and her brother took it and sold it sometime during the night. Rachelle claimed her brother returned the day after the barbeque and told her what he had done. Then she said Harrell had a different gun at the barbeque, and he brandished it at her other brother and tried to steal his camera in payment for the gun that had been stolen earlier in the day, noting that the brother who sold the weapon wasn't at the barbecue. It became a challenge for investigators to try and follow her story. Unfortunately, this is typical of what detectives face in these types of crimes—convoluted stories that have to be unraveled like a spider web. This confusion is what makes solving these cases so arduous and time-consuming.

Rachelle then said the barbeque was the day the body was found, but she corrected herself. It was the day Michelle left with Erica in the stroller. But, first, she said she didn't see Michelle after that until December. This time, she said, Michelle came to Naomi's house late on the day of the barbecue.

By early afternoon, the reporting detective had Rachelle Allendale start over. "Take it from the top" with Rachelle was like opening a new box of Cracker Jack—you never knew what you'd find when you got to the bottom of it. She was asked to go over all the events she could remember, starting with when Harrell, Michelle, and the two little girls moved into her home. Rachelle began by stating that in March 2001, Harrell was hiding from police after cutting a woman's finger off. At first, Harrell stayed at Naomi's house. However, Michelle showed up shortly after when they moved into Rachelle's house.

She said that Michelle called Erica's grandmother and made plans to bring the child back to Kansas City a few weeks later. Rachelle accompanied Michelle to Muskogee to pick up the child. They took a bus and made the trip, staying overnight in Muskogee. She noted that Erica broke into tears when the little girl laid eyes on Harrell. Not long after Erica arrived, Michelle and Harrell began fighting. Harrell didn't mind an audience. He beat Michelle, leaving bruises and other injuries, and he'd do it in front of Rachelle. Rachelle stood by and didn't do anything to help Michelle or get her police assistance.

Rachelle described drug use by the couple while they stayed with her. She knew the distinctive odors that crack cocaine and PCP gave off when smoked and explained how they would walk around the house with "sticks" or cigarettes dipped in PCP. She went on to say that occasionally she would smoke "blunts" (cigarettes laced with marijuana) with Michelle "to chill." So perhaps watching Harrell beating his girlfriend and her child was a little stressful for Rachelle Allendale!

She spoke of how the fighting continued for an entire week, and Erica got caught up as a prisoner of war in the battle waging between her mother and Harrell. Although she was fighting with him, Michelle wasn't so angry that she wouldn't delegate her parental responsibilities back to Harrell. On the contrary, she let him do what she should have done and in a manner that no one should have done. Rachelle recalled when Michelle told Harrell to whip Erica because the child had wet her pants. Harrell went into Rachelle's room, retrieved a wire hanger, and promptly went into the back room where a frightened Erica stood. She heard Erica getting beaten with the hanger. She said it went on for over 10 minutes. While they remained in her home, Rachelle Allendale said any time Erica would cry, Harrell would whip her, and she knew of several times that he used a belt on the little girl. She noted that Harrell would beat the child until she vomited. She confirmed that she did witness physical abuse and saw the injuries that resulted. The scars and bruises the detectives found on the dead child's body were suspected to be the results of abuse. After hearing Allendale's story, the physical evidence suddenly made sense, and the puzzle pieces fell together. The picture it gave was a harrowing image of a ragged, pitiful child, reminiscent of 19th century Dickensian tale, difficult to comprehend in 21st-century America.

In an apparent attempt to distance herself from her tenants, Rachelle told officers that the only child punishment she would allow in her home was for a child to take a "time out" sitting in a chair in the corner. When detectives inquired why she failed to call the police because of the domestic disturbances or the abuse of the child, she would only say, "I don't know."

Changing the subject, Rachelle went on to talk about a loud crashing sound from the back bedroom that she had heard a few days later. Erica began crying again, and Harrell was cursing at her when a deafening noise came from the rear of the house. Rachelle hollered, "What was that?" Michelle yelled back that a speaker had fallen over. Rachelle said the crashing noises happened once before when Harrell was stumbling around after using PCP and he couldn't walk, so she took Michelle's response as factual. This time, however, Erica would never leave the room on her own again, and Michelle would offer no plausible explanation as to why the child had suddenly gone silent. As a result, Rachelle only saw her once more; two days later, the child appeared asleep in a stroller. Michelle was pushing Erica and her sister down the street, walking toward Jackson Street.

She indicated that the day she saw Michelle go for a walk was the same as the barbecue at her mother's house—the same story she told detectives early. However, this time she said Michelle cried, saying that Mrs. Brown had picked up Erica earlier that day and that she would never see the little girl again. Michelle stayed one more night at Rachelle Allendale's after that. Rachelle wouldn't see Michelle again until December 2001, after the birth of Michelle's baby boy fathered by Harrell.

Rachelle veered off course one more time, stating that she saw Michelle at one of the weekly prayer vigils that Alvin Brooks and the Precious Doe Committee held near the area where the body had been found, appearing as just another face in the crowd. She said that Michelle approached Alvin Brooks and said, "Whoever did this needs to pay," and she helped pass out the "Do You Know Me?" flyers that the committee made up to help locate anyone who might know something about the case.

History shows that killers often do go back to the scene of the crime, if not to revel in their deeds as serial killers usually do, but to blend in, hide in broad daylight, secreting themselves under the glow of streetlamps, in an attempt to cast off the specter of guilt that lingers about them, if guilt is felt by those otherwise soul-less creatures devoid of conscience or remorse.

An adage in investigations suggests always investigating your source because it has been proven that suspects will often be at the scene when the police arrive, often to insinuate themselves into the investigation. They do so by providing helpful information because 1) they get a thrill out of talking to the police, reveling in the fact that police have no idea who they are at that point, or 2) in an attempt to assess what the police might know about the crime. One example is the Ali Kemp murder case, where the suspect, Benjamin Appleby, remained at the scene and was standing in the crowd where police had interviewed him.

Rachelle Allendale wasn't able to tell the detectives anything else. Although she was guilty of the crime of silence for standing by and allowing her tenants to abuse a child in her presence and failing to intervene or report the abuse, she was allowed to leave. The detectives gave both Rachelle Allendale and Naomi Allendale a ride back home. That must have been an uncomfortable trip for all concerned.

Pictures

Spraying Luminol at Crime Scene
Courtesy of Kansas City, Missouri Police Department

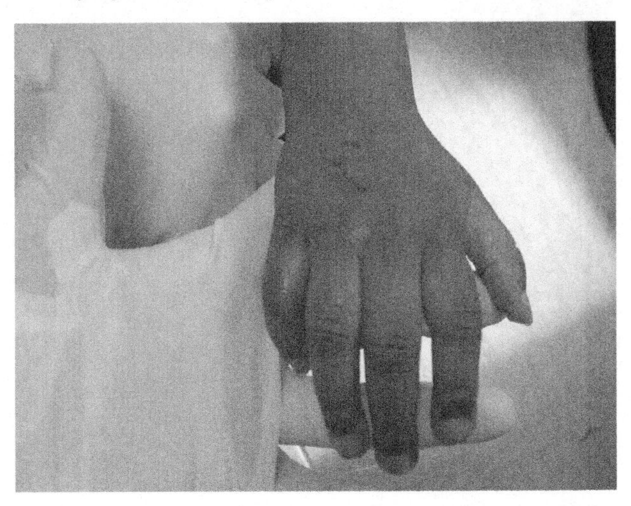

Precious Doe Autopsy Photo
Courtesy of David Bernard

Exhumation of Precious Doe
Courtesy of David Bernard

Precious Doe Reconstruction
Courtesy of David Bernard

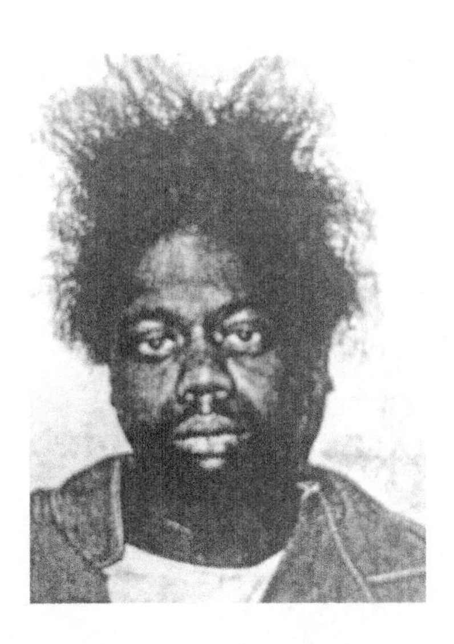

Harrell Johnson Booking Photo
Courtesy of Kansas City, Missouri Police Department

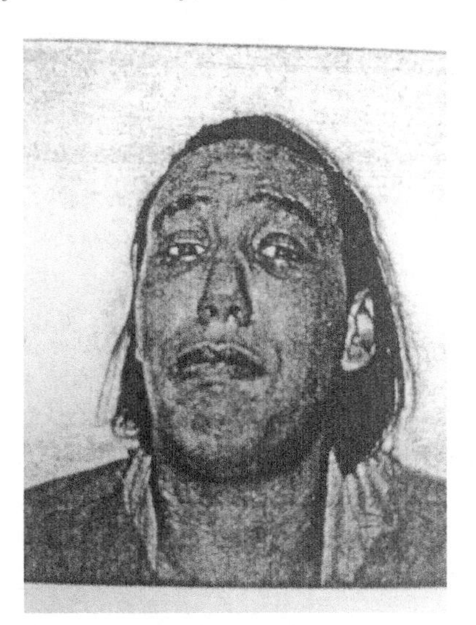

Michelle Johnson Booking Photo
Courtesy of Kansas City, Missouri Police Department

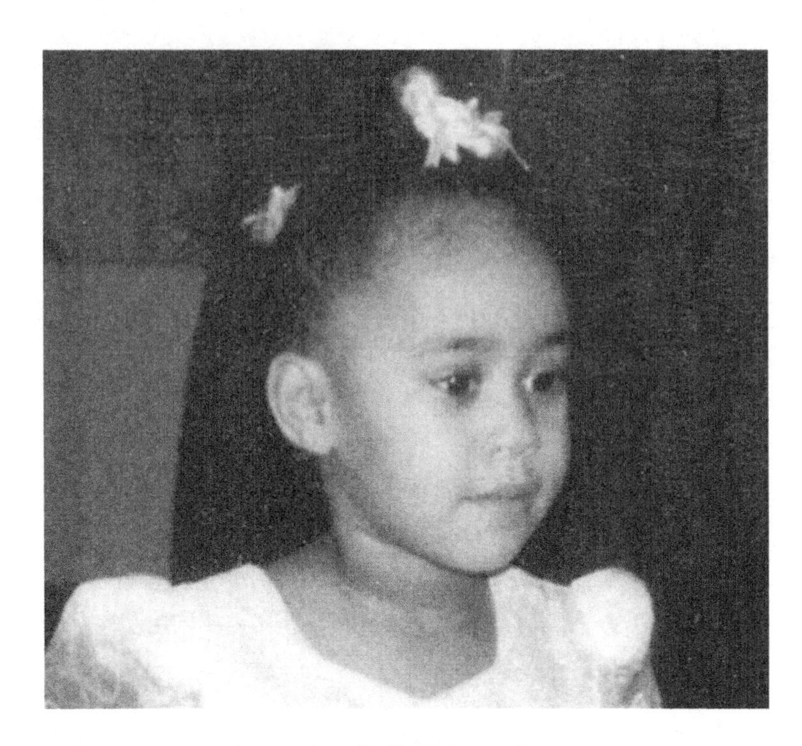

Erica Michelle Marie Green
Courtesy of Betty Brown

She Had Known Love

While Rachelle Allendale was rambling on to the investigative team at the police station, other detectives interviewed Nancy Jackson, one of Betty Brown's daughters, at the hospital where she worked.

Nancy had been a foster mother to six children, and her mother also decided to take in foster children. She recalled that Betty Brown took Erica in as a temporary foster child until Michelle was released from prison. Michelle didn't exercise her right to reclaim Erica and only saw the little girl once in a while for short periods. She never brought anything for the child and didn't offer to give Betty any money to help care for her little girl. Shortly before she took Erica for the last time, Michelle began taking her to a motel for an overnight visit a few times. This was the only "care" Erica received from her mother. She went on to say that she didn't like Michelle or how she treated Erica. Nancy called her "pushy and difficult." She was disgusted that Michelle had given birth to a drug-addicted baby after she had Erica.

Michelle would insist that Betty give her the child's WIC vouchers, but the foster mother would never concede to her demands. What Nancy said bothered her most was Erica's behavior when Michelle came around. The terrified child would cry and beg to stay with Betty. Erica would fight as best a little girl could to resist going with Michelle. When she was finally returned to Betty, she would pull away, not allowing anyone to touch her hair. She'd jump as if startled or hurt if anyone suddenly tried to hug her. Her behaviors were classic signs of someone who had experienced abuse.

Nancy told how her sister, Dorothy, loved little Erica and called her "my baby" and how emotional Dorothy got when Michelle failed to bring her back after taking her for a so-called "family reunion" in Oklahoma City. She was at work that day and didn't know if Michelle had anyone else with her. She only knew that her mother would not give Michelle any money and only a few clothes for three-year-old Erica—supposedly just enough for the weekend. She did know that Michelle called Betty and asked for money, but Betty refused until Michelle brought the child back. As we know now, no money and no child exchanged hands.

Nancy told detectives that she didn't know anything about Erica's family other than that she had a grandmother that lived in Chicago. She went on to say that she didn't think anything of Erica not coming back because Michelle told Betty that she had left Erica with her mother in Illinois. It seemed like a reasonable answer at the time. It had been a pattern for Michelle to leave her children in her mother's care and return to Harrell. Nancy said she never saw Michelle again after Erica was taken for the "reunion." Still, Betty said she saw Michelle once in a McDonald's in Muskogee after Erica was taken away. Michelle apparently stuck by her story of little Erica with Granny in Chi-Town.

Brother, Can You Spare A Dime?

When the murder investigation began in May 2005, the State of Missouri Department of Social Services initiated an investigation into Michelle Johnson's assistance to Erica. They determined that Michelle collected welfare for Erica from May 2001 through August 2001, so she committed welfare fraud and stealing in Missouri. Social Services also learned that Michelle and Harrell had been obtaining services from the Illinois Department of Public Aid. A letter was sent requesting information on this as a matter of routine. What was uncovered was that Michelle was indeed collecting assistance—for Erica. She entered the welfare office and filled out paperwork as though the little girl required Illinois' help. Michelle applied in May 2004 and continued collecting it until the discovery of Erica's identity in May 2005, and her claim was canceled on June 1, 2005. Harrell also claimed benefits as a part of this little charade. He and Michelle were charged in Illinois with felonies for providing false information and having collected benefits in excess of $10,000. The Illinois investigator and her supervisor were all over it and expedited this case the minute it was discovered. It was refreshing to see that at least there was decisive action on the part of Public Aid in Illinois to hold the couple accountable for such an outrageous act. What is also unfortunate is that there were genuinely impoverished people in Illinois who were deprived of this money. When they collected the money, Michelle and Harrell weren't even in the State. They were in Oklahoma when this all went down, getting public assistance from the good folks in the Sooner State. Erica's killers took profits from three separate jurisdictions, knowing they had murdered the little girl. It was blood money, pure and simple.

Amazing Disgrace

The second memorial for Erica was held while David was in Oklahoma and was lovely, spontaneous, and uneventful. Again, it was held at the Metropolitan Missionary Baptist Church, and this time it was a home-going service that could honor the child whose identity was now known. Following the service, attendees traveled to the park at 59th and Kensington for a small ceremony led by Alvin Brooks with songs and prayers.

On May 15, 2005, just days after the case was solved, the community celebrated Erica's birthday in the park that had become the gathering place for all things related to the Precious Doe case. There were pony rides, balloons, and a clown, but tragically, the birthday girl would be notably absent from the festivities.

While this transpired, two Kansas City detectives and six members of the Jackson County, Missouri, Sheriff's Department had the dubious task of ensuring the two suspects were returned safely to stand trial and avoid being the main event at a vigilante execution at 59th and Kensington. There was a makeshift memorial there, and it would not have taken much for an angry mob from the neighborhood to have erected a spot sufficient for spontaneous capital punishment.

Two days later, Harrell and Michelle were arraigned. Harrell had been cleaned up and appeared slightly better than the wild-haired, crazy-eyed killer that his mug shots captured shortly after his arrest.

On June 6, 2001, another child homicide victim would be buried in Kansas City. Hers was an eight-year-old case that had been solved, but her body would not be recovered until years later. In the Precious Doe case, there was a body with no name. In this case, there was a murdered child, but her remains were only recovered three months before the decapitated child in Kansas City was discovered. There are many parallels between these cases; vulnerable single mothers, histories of abuse, drug addiction, poverty, and violent boyfriends who directed their frustrations at a small child. Telling the story of Kansas City child murders without sharing the details of the 1993 case would be a disservice as it emphasizes the impact these cases have on families, communities, and the dedicated detectives who work tirelessly to solve these crimes. Her name defined who she was and what she represented. She was Angel Hart.

Angel Hart was another faceless innocent mired at the bottom of the welfare ravine. It would be many years before she would be recovered in what would be genuinely a "valley of the shadow of death." Her brief existence was only discovered when California welfare workers wanted to see her in person when her mother applied for assistance for her five children and only four were physically present. It was at this time that authorities discovered the five-year-old girl was missing. This observation was pretty good for welfare workers, given their national track record of losing children in the accountability abyss that is our "system." It was not known then that Kansas City's 1020 Homicide Squad would have one particularly notorious case a few years later that would have been blessed with this much accuracy or attention from social services. In the 1990s, portions of the Missouri social services system were inefficiently run, and the word service was used loosely. In Angel Hart's case,

Missouri child welfare was an oxymoron, if there ever was one.

Why do they always wait until the evening shift to notice that someone is missing or dead? That's how Sgt. Bernard ended up with the case. He was working nights, and the squad got the call from the police department in El Cajon, California. Last known address: a low-rent motel located ½ in Kansas City and ½ in Independence, Missouri. Room 60 of the Green Crest Motel on East 40 highway happened to have the bathroom situated on the Kansas City side of the building. So that's where the crime occurred. He assigned Detectives Dean Allen and Joe Crayon to the case (yes, Crayon is his real name, not something from Film Noir). Joe Crayon, Angel Hart, Gary Christian, children's alphabet. Truth is often stranger than fiction.

Angel's mother broke down and told authorities that her boyfriend had beaten and drowned Angel in the motel bathroom. She said his reason for assaulting Angel was because the terrified little girl could not recite her ABCs correctly, confusing the order of the letters I and J. After killing the child. Christian bought a Rubbermaid container and stuffed her body in it, covering it with cement. They packed up the container and the other children and headed to California. This excursion turned into a modern-day Grapes of Wrath—WRATH being the operative word. Somewhere along the way, the boyfriend dumped the container down a hill on a deserted stretch of desert highway. The challenge that the detectives faced was to do an investigation that prosecutors could build a strong case on to get a conviction without a body. The boyfriend was arrested and extradited. He confessed to the killing and copped a plea of second-degree murder in turn for cooperating and taking detectives to the place where the body was dumped. The score was Christians 1, Angels zip. Only Christian took them to the wrong road on the wrong highway in the wrong desert in the wrong state. The highway had recently been re-routed, and it all seemed plausible. But no heavy equipment could find her because they looked in the wrong place.

Gary Lynn Christian was 33 years old in April of 1994 when he was arrested in San Diego County for the February 22, 1993, murder of Angel Hart. He was initially held on a $255,000 bond for second-degree murder and first-degree assault, but charges were upgraded to first-degree murder as new evidence came to light. No bail for Gary. He had outstanding warrants for miscellaneous mischief, but that was just a drop in the bathtub.

Angela Melton was arrested and charged with hindering prosecution, child endangerment, and stealing. She was only 22 years old and had five kids, if you count the dead one and the one she announced she was pregnant with when she was arraigned in Kansas City. The prosecutor filed the child endangerment count because Melton continued letting Christian access her two biological children living in California. Adding to the counts against her, prosecutors charged her with stealing because she received more than $150 in Medicaid and Aid to Dependent Children in Angel's name in the two months they remained in Missouri after Angel's murder. Despite all this, Melton was confident that she would not face charges related to Angel's death. She considered herself "a great parent." She had one dead child, two wards of the State of California, one in the custody of Missouri, and was pregnant with another that would become Missouri's responsibility once it was born.

Jackson County prosecutors begged to differ with Melton. They argued that Melton had the opportunity to at least tell police about the murder even if she couldn't have done it right after it happened due to her alleged fear of Christian. After all, she had fought with Christian before the attack on Angel—Christian's actions were a blatant retaliation toward Angela. It was a classic "I'll pick on her to piss you off" mentality. She did nothing to intercede as Angel fought for her life and screamed, "Help me, Mommy!" So now Angela was facing 23 years in prison—more years than she had even been alive.

Melton admitted that she was in the hotel room when Christian assaulted and killed Angel in February 1993. She also acknowledged that Kansas City police officers contacted both her and Christian in April 1993 when they received a report from a relative claiming that Angel was being abused by her so-called parents. However, Melton told the police that she had never observed Gary hurting her children. Did anyone ask to see the kids to confirm their well-being? This failure to physically observe and account for each child would be an issue that would come up in the Precious Doe case. These are such simple questions to ask, but ones with such devastating consequences when gone unanswered. Shortly after this interaction with the police, Christian packed up the "family" and headed for California. Angela Melton had ample opportunity to tell the police and she failed to do so. Instead, Melton went with Christian across the country. They ended up in El Cajon. Melton went to great lengths—and distances—to be with Christian, but she was now the Jackson County prosecutor's star witness against him. This same scenario would also play out in the Precious Doe case.

When she met Gary Christian, Angela Melton was already a train wreck, yet she chose to live with him in late 1992. At only 20 years old, she had three kids by two different fathers —the paternity of Angel remains questionable to this day. Gary must have seemed like a port in a storm, but he turned out worse than the hurricane from which she was trying to take refuge. She weathered beatings and other forms of abuse at the hands of an alcoholic, Gary, but she didn't know how or where to go to get away from him. Due to her dysfunctional lifestyle, Angela had burned most bridges with family and friends. Had she given the kids to any of them for long-term care, they might have been more willing to take her in.

A Kansas City Star reporter quoted Melton saying, "I wanted to leave, but I didn't know what to do. I stayed there mostly for his boys. They just needed a mother in their life, and I was there. I thought I could be the best thing that happened to them." She was pregnant with her child by Gary Christian in 1993 when Angel was murdered, yet another similarity between the Angel Hart and Precious Doe murders. She was also pregnant, but not by Christian when she was arrested and extradited to Missouri for her part in Angel's death. It's not funny, but it brings to mind the old Bill Cosby joke about how he disciplined his kids. He said he'd tell them, "I brought you into this world, and I can take you back out. I can make another one that looks just like you." Angela Melton—the Xerox of motherhood.

The California child protection folks did a respectable job accounting for the kids and bringing the case to light. However, it was still a reasonably dysfunctional operation. They permitted Angela to see her kids during the week and every other weekend and enrolled her in parenting classes. Unfortunately, little progress was made in Melton's ability to parent children, and one has to wonder what authorities were thinking by endorsing this arrangement. Cases like Angel Hart and Precious Doe show that reunification is not always in the children's best interest. Attempting to school Angela Melton in an area she could not grasp, with no desire or ability to nurture, was like teaching a pig to sing. It wastes your time and annoys the pig.

Before the murder, Melton's children were the center of a botched State DFS investigation in late December. What played out was a ping-pong match between DFS and the family members and physicians who reported the abuse to the police department that shuttled the children back and forth. The abuse was reported and documented on December 21 after Melton took one of her boys to the emergency room of Children's Mercy Hospital. He was severely malnourished at six months old and had an infected rash covering his lower abdomen and scrotum. In addition, his weight was less than half of what it should have been. The hospital staff placed a hotline call to DFS to report the abuse, and he was put into State custody. Despite this, the DFS worker determined Christian and Melton would make suitable candidates for the State's family preservation program, where they'd get in-home parenting classes. Family reunification was her recommendation to the court, so the other children were returned to them. They were teaching the pig to sing again.

A week after the emergency room trip, a hearing for the hotline report was held, and the court decided that the baby needed to remain with the State. The DFS worker did not attend the hearing, nor was she aware that family members were in discussions with another DFS worker about Angel's claims about her abuse. The DFS worker had dusted her hands of the issue for the time being. It was December 28—the day that family preservation was to visit the Melton-Christian home for the first time, so she wasn't concerned. Perhaps she would have been concerned had she known that Angel wasn't there—and apparently, no one from DFS even asked about her.

With the agreement of the other DFS worker, Melton allowed family friend Christine (Kemmerer) Stevens to take Angel with her. Over the years, Melton had allowed Christine, her cousin Tammy Jackson, and even her own mother—who had a criminal record for narcotics —to take Angel for brief periods of time. So finally, Angel was safe with Christine, but not for long.

While at Stevens' home, Angel apparently awoke from a nightmare and told Stevens that Christian would kill her. Then she began to tell the story of how Christian tortured her. She described how he beat her, tied her up, hung her upside down, and held her face underwater because she wouldn't recite her ABCs correctly. According to Stevens, Angel would say "JHI" instead of "HIJ." Stevens notified Jackson of the allegations and took Angel to a safe house for women and children. Angel repeated her story to the staff. In the meantime, Tammy Jackson went to Melton's house and confronted Melton in the presence of the social worker overseeing the family preservation process. At least DFS kept showing up, but they didn't do anything right.

Melton and Christian were angry and told Stevens to bring the child back. When she refused and instead took her back to the shelter, Melton called the police. Despite the cries and pleading of the desperate child, Stevens had to allow them to take her back or face arrest. Angel was so hysterical that she vomited. Finally, it was agreed that Tammy Jackson's husband would transport Angel back to Melton to spare the child any more trauma than she was already experiencing. Stevens, however, wasn't giving up, and neither was Jackson.

Stevens called the original DFS worker the following day and told her story. On December 30, the DFS worker met with Angel and took her into a separate room at the Melton-Christian home. She asked Angel if she was abused, and Angel said she got spanked. She recanted the story of being hung upside down in the closet, and the DFS worker took her at her word. She was only five years old and terrified. A professional should have known that a child victim of abuse will recant out of fear or a misplaced need to protect the abuser, generally the caregiver. The DFS worker failed to interview either of Christian's sons, older than Angel, who witnessed the child's suffering. Those boys were also violently abused by their father. Why she believed Melton and Christian remains a mystery. Her recommendation would remain that Angel should stay with the family.

In a twisted act of fate, while this was happening, Stevens, Jackson, and a shelter staff member were at court, getting a judge to grant temporary custody of Angel and her 18-month-old brother to Jackson. Police served the order early that evening and ended up arresting Christian. He went off like a rocket.

The children were taken back to the emergency room at Children's Mercy Hospital and were seen by a physician. The telltale bruises consistent with abuse were documented when the baby was examined. Angel didn't have any outward signs of abuse, but the story she told the physician was just as traumatic as what showed up on the other child. It was all documented, and the physician, convinced Angel was truthful, called the hotline. Tammy Jackson took the children home, and for less than 12 hours, they were safe once more.

The next day, the children were back in the throes of the ping-pong match. The DFS worker learned of the hotline call and decided that the new court order didn't allow the family preservation program to start. Despite a phone call from the CMH physician supporting Angel's claims, DFS went back to the judge and persuaded him to reverse his decision based on her recommendation. Somehow, the slurred words of two low-life druggies were more credible than a pediatric medical professional whose specialty was recognizing telltale—and often remote—signs of abuse. The social worker could not see the blinding glimpse of the obvious shining into her eyes. The judge signed Angel Hart's death warrant. Later, he would be asked about the case and claim he didn't remember the details. He can tell you all about Star Trek if you ask him. Talk about screwed-up priorities. Perhaps Angel would have been easier to remember if she looked like a science fiction character. The saddest part of this is that he remained on the bench in Jackson County even after the story of Angel Hart was brought to light. It is a tragic reminder that voters need to look at who they're re-electing and not just hit the button for judges.

On New Year's Eve in 1992, Angel Hart was transported, along with her brother, back to the location of her torture via a police car. While a bright 1993 was dawning for others, this was the beginning of the end for Angel Hart.

Like Precious Doe, Angel's treatment brings to mind an *HBO* special called *Shelter Dogs*. A New York State kennel deals with canines who cannot be reintroduced into society because of behaviors they cannot overcome due to abuse and neglect. One particularly aggressive Cocker Spaniel had to be euthanized because there was no hope of mainstreaming him for adoption. Yet, before he was put down, kennel staff took him for a final car ride and gave him the last treat of a hamburger purchased at the local McDonald's restaurant. How ironic that even a dog's dignity is respected in many parts of the nation, yet children continue to be expendable, treated as no more than disposable life forms. Where was a glimmer of dignity for Angel Hart? Where was her Happy Meal? The innocent little girl wasn't even treated like a dog.

The next few weeks were typical in the Melton-Christian household: fights, drinking, and child neglect. Angel's abuse was occurring more frequently. She bore the brunt of Christian's frustration. Finally, the family was evicted from their home and moved into the Green Crest Motel. There was one other witness besides Melton on the night of Angel's murder, one of Christian's sons. According to his statement, he was in the bathroom when Christian began drowning Angel. He watched as Christian put her in the bathtub and held her head underwater. The boy described how his father would pull the child's head up and, when she cried out, "Help me, Mommy," would push her back underwater. Finally, he said Christian picked up the child, carried her out, and handed her to Melton. He described her appearance as "limp like she was asleep, and her face was pale."

Angel started going into seizures, and Melton tried to give her CPR. Melton and Christian finally attempted to get her help, but she died in the car on the way to the hospital. Christian told Melton that DFS would take the kids for sure if they went on to the hospital. They returned to the motel, and Christian took off with the deceased child. No one ever saw her again.

Stevens and Jackson never gave up on Angel. They again reported the abuse to the police, resulting in Christian and Melton being questioned in April 1993, two months after Angel's murder. The inquiry was enough to scare them into leaving town, dragging a total of 4 kids, a few meager belongings, and a blue Rubbermaid container Christian retrieved from a storage facility in Independence.

The trek to California didn't work out well for the Donner Party, and the Melton-Christian "family" didn't fare much better. Settling in El Cajon, California, the cycle of drinking, abuse, and dysfunction continued. Christian beat Melton, and she finally had enough, calling the police and getting him arrested. She didn't have legal custody of his two sons, so California social services became involved. California may be broke, but they did know how to operate a welfare system, at least investigating child welfare. When they inquired about the other children, they learned that the youngest child was supposed to be in the custody of the State of Missouri. So they snatched him up and sent him back to foster care in Kansas City. Then they asked about Angel. Angel WHO? Melton said she was with family in the Midwest. Hmm. Not so fast. The investigation would pull a thread unraveling a bizarre story that could only be true.

When Christian was released from jail on the domestic violence case, he left a message on Melton's answering machine threatening to pick up "a little package from the desert" and planned to leave it on her social worker's desk. The "little package" was Angel. This threat occurred on October 24, and by the 27th, Melton had gone to the El Cajon police and confessed to Det. Tom Buhl that Christian had killed Angel and dumped her off the side of the highway somewhere between California and Arizona. According to Melton, Christian threw out something she loved—her daughter. Hearing this story, Buhl notified the welfare workers, and they, in turn, told the Kansas City Police Department. The receipt of this call is where Sgt. Bernard and the 1020 squad enter the picture.

Buhl did his best to locate Angel. He, like David, was obsessed with the child's disappearance. Buhl and a partner searched over 1,200 miles for her. He had notified all Arizona law enforcement agencies about what Melton had described. No leads. No container. No Angel. One key piece of information Buhl documented and shared with Kansas City police was the transcript of the telephone message that Gary Christian left on Melton's answering machine on October 24, 1993. The following is the transcribed recording exactly as initially spoken by Christian:

"Okay, Angie, that was the last fucking time I'm gonna put up with your hanging up on me. I'm going out to the fucking desert tonight, baby, and I'm getting that little package, and I'm bringing it back to somebody. I'm fucking sick and tired of your fucking bullshit; you can stay there and suck Bob's dick for all I care. I'm done. I'm through. This was it. You fucking came into my life, Angie; I had a house, I had everything, you fucking came into my life, and you fucking destroyed it. Now you got my fucking kids taken away from me. Well, Linda will get them back. I didn't never tell you this, but she's got joint custody of them fucking kids. When we got divorced, they gave her joint custody. All she's got to do is walk up there and show her fucking paper, and she's got them, and she walks off with them. In the meantime, I'm gone, Angel's sitting at the DFS worker's fucking desk, and you're fucking gone."

Angela was 15 years old when Angel was born. She wasn't exactly sure who the father was. She named two different men, but no paternity tests were ever conducted, so no one knows conclusively. Perhaps that's better, given Angela's track record. Angel was born three months prematurely, and her heart wasn't fully developed. She was kept in the neonatal intensive care unit, undergoing surgery to repair her heart. She never caught a break, that little girl, but miraculously she survived despite it all. She had a genuinely miraculous ANGEL HEART.

In 1995, Melton finally filed for divorce from Micheal Melton while incarcerated in the Jackson County jail. Perhaps the convenience of court-appointed attorneys makes tidying up your personal life a little more convenient. In the summer of that year, Christian began cooperating with the Jackson County prosecutor but only on the condition that he could plead to the lesser charge of second-degree murder. In return, he would show them where he dumped Angel's body. It wasn't the outcome that family and friends wanted, but having an answer was critical if there was to be any hope of closure to this mystery. At least Angel could come home and be appropriately buried instead of lying alone in the desert. Tammy Jackson testified and agreed to the lesser charge if, as a condition, they could get Angel's remains back. It was a painful but reasonable decision.

City detectives took Christian to Arizona, where they initiated the search for Angel. Christian described an area near the California border by a Native American Reservation. He had panicked when he thought state border patrols would look in his car. He dumped her out and drove away. As part of the search, they found a broken cube of concrete with what appeared to be the impression of a child's arm. Christian had poured cement over Angel's body when he placed her in the bin. Maybe this was it. There was nothing conclusive in the test results on what they found.

Road work had changed the area dramatically, so nothing looked the same. Christian couldn't find what he claimed he could. He told the officers that the day after Angel died, he and Melton took Angel's body to the storage locker he rented in Independence, Missouri. Christian stated he went to the Builders Surplus Storage on 40 Highway, purchased the Rubbermaid container and a bag of Quikcrete cement mix, and returned to the storage locker, where he mixed up the cement. He went on to say that he poured a layer of cement into the bottom of the container. Angel, dressed in a pink sweatsuit, was wrapped up in Melton's gray-colored trench coat and placed in a black trash bag. He said Angel was in a fetal position (with knees up against her chest) and that he put her upright in the container. Melton held her in place while Christian poured the remaining concrete into layers around Angel's lifeless body. She was paralyzed in concrete, frozen in time.

Bernard didn't give up on the case, nor did Tom Buhl. A year after Christian failed to point out Angel's whereabouts, Buhl went so far as to come from California to Kansas City and assist a hypnotist he brought in who was going to try and elicit new information from Christian. Jog his subconscious, if you will. Christian didn't have a conscience, so maybe he had something buried away, even if it wasn't remorse. It couldn't hurt anyway, and the authorities from the prison and the prosecutor's office allowed it. Two hours and a bunch of money later, nothing, nada, zippo.

In February of 2001, eight years after her death, a California woman stumbled upon the remains of Angel Hart. While taking photographs in the desert, she saw what appeared to be a concrete block, charred from a wildfire that had burned the area, and she kicked it with her foot. It broke open and revealed the bones of a small child. It was about 150 feet from where Tom Buhl searched, but it had been concealed by the brush which burned away during the wildfire. It is said that God works in His own good time, and Angel's destiny follows the timetable of the Lord.

It appeared that Angel could finally come home. But it would not be that easy. There was no peace in Angel's life, and she wasn't getting any closer to rest in eternal peace just yet. When Melton learned of the discovery, she demanded to have the remains so that she could cremate them and keep them with her. But, of course, she had done a pretty lousy job so far, so what would make her think she could protect her now?

The family was up in arms, and so were the Kansas City detectives that worked her case. The prosecutor's office tried to block Melton from getting the remains. Tammy Jackson had made arrangements with a local cemetery that donated a plot so Angel could be buried with dignity, but now another stumbling block stood in the path to eternal rest for this poor child. Jackson was livid, and Christine Stevens was inconsolable. Authorities needed to take Angel out of the fray and get her home. Handling her remains had gone from the sublime to the ridiculous, and it had to stop. Finally, Melton agreed to sign away her rights to the child's remains, and once the DNA results were confirmed, Tammy Jackson could move forward with the funeral arrangements. Maybe.

The DNA results came two weeks after the 1020 Squad picked up another notorious murder case involving another murdered little girl. This time detectives had a body, but there were no suspects, no identification, and no one looking to claim her. God deliver us—here we go again. There was no time to absorb the impact of finding Angel Hart. Another precious little girl was murdered, and he'd carry her on his back until he could get her case solved.

As with everything about Angel's case, the comedy of errors continued. Part of Angel's remains had been sent to Canadian DNA experts for identification. When they returned the package containing some of her bones and teeth, the remains got lost in the mail. If ever there was a case of insult added to injury, this was it. The family was beside themselves and insisted that something be done to prevent further mishaps. Finally, a tenacious Jackson County prosecutor who handled the case decided to fly to California and retrieve the remains so she could bring Angel home. Finally, on June 6, 2001, Angel Hart was laid to rest at Mount Washington Cemetery. Sgt. Bernard took time off long enough from his new child victim case to go and attend that service. Balloons were released at the conclusion of the service. As these floated up to the clouds, it was hoped that perhaps she could see them from some celestial vantage point and know that she was the angel who held a place in the hearts of those who never knew her but loved her just the same.

Angela Melton served four years for her part in Angel's death. Gary Christian continues to serve his life sentence at the Eastern Reception Diagnostic and Correctional Center in Bonne Terre, Missouri. The division investigator assigned to the Angel Hart case no longer works for the agency. Tom Buhl suffered a stroke in 1999 and had to retire from the El Cajon Police Department. David Bernard was now investigating the beheading murder of an unidentified three-year-old known only as "Precious Doe". Angel Lea Hart is buried at Mount Washington Cemetery.

Angel, Erica, and other innocent children slip between the cracks in a fractured child protection system. Angel's mother suffered from the "disease to please," exposing her child to the wrath of a boyfriend who killed her for not knowing her ABCs. Tragically, an eerily similar fate had befallen "Precious Doe".

The Kindness of Strangers

The "Precious Doe" case was beginning to reach its tentacles throughout the community. On June 3, 2005, a concerned citizen called the Homicide Unit. The Emergency Assistance Coordinator of the Cathedral of Immaculate Conception noticed the name "Harrell Johnson" during an audit of church records. He had seen Johnson being identified on local news reports as being charged with the "Precious Doe" murder. He said he had information that he thought would benefit the case. The caller related that Johnson came to the church on April 21, 2005, claiming the need to get back to work in Muskogee after staying with relatives in Kansas City but needed funds to buy a bus ticket. Johnson said he worked at Kid's World Day Care and that his employer could verify it. The caller said staff at the Cathedral contacted Kid's World and received a fax confirmation of his employment, so he was given a Greyhound bus voucher. The caller also agreed to fax all the related documents to the Homicide Unit for the case file. It was disconcerting to think that Harrell worked at a daycare center. Oklahoma childcare regulations included a background check for criminal history, but somehow, he slipped between the cracks.

As it turned out, the concerned citizen was Paul Kim, a former Kansas City, Missouri, police officer injured in the line of duty. Paul is the kind of individual who always steps up and does the right thing. How many years and how much pain would have been spared to so many individuals if Harrell's own mother, grandfather, the landlady, or a host of others had come forward with what they knew?

In Heavenly Peace

On August 18, 2005, the final burial service for Erica Green was held at Memorial Park Cemetery. This event would allow her disinterred remains to be reburied now that the case had been solved. Kansas City Mayor Pro-Tem Alvin Brooks, Danny Phillips, Sgt. Bernard, and his 19-year-old son, Matthew, were the pallbearers of Erica's new casket that the Batesville Casket Company and Park Lawn Funeral Home had donated. In addition, there would be a new headstone, one donated by Kansas City Monument Company, with Erica's name, dates of birth, and death, along with the inscription, "Our angel Precious Doe. We love you". The marker would forever link Erica Green to "Precious Doe", a name the little girl was known by for more months than she had been alive.

Mrs. Brown and her family came back to Kansas City for this service. Sue Stiltner and Mary Manhein flew to Kansas City for the service and bought the dress that Erica would wear when she was buried for the second time. By this time, Sue and Mary were entrenched in the case, and both wanted to be a part of Erica's final journey. Death also works in mysterious ways.

Sue also bought her a small, dainty cross befitting her stature. Just as they had done to pick the perfect clothes, Sgt. Bernard's wife searched store after store to find the right teddy bear to be Erica's companion in the afterlife. She was also asked to write a poem to be read as part of the memorial service and to prepare programs that were given to all the attendees. Sue and Mary undertook the grim task of dressing the little girl for her final burial. Again, she was being readied to cross over on her final journey to a better place. Mary had prepared the skull for burial, removing the exterior clay mask that gave the head the features that revealed Erica to the world. Her skull would be placed with her body, and she would be whole once again. It would, however, still be long before anyone but Erica could begin to rest.

The following is the poem that was read at Erica's memorial:

Adopted Angel

Now we lay you down in peace
In the arms of Mother Earth
Safe from those who caused you harm
And never knew your worth.
We struggled to make sense of this
And each in some small way
Took you as our own to love
And care for through this day.
From the art of man and Manhein
We came to know your smile.
We didn't know your name or age
But we loved you all the while.
What was tossed away with no remorse
Was precious all the more
To those of us whose lives you touched
And changed forever more.
The last four years are put to rest
With closure and relief
A healing may begin at last
From hurt beyond belief.
God has smiled upon your face
You're brightened by His light
Upon your head a halo glows
A new star in the night.
Your identity revealed now
Shows us your name and face
We part as if we knew you well
As we bring you to this place
Where you can rest your little head
Adorned now in a crown
Safe and blessed into that good night
We gently lay you down.

At that time, Sgt. Bernard wrote a letter to his squad to acknowledge their commitment as unsung heroes to a job that never ends.

"This notice is to express my personal gratitude for the effort and dedication you have shown to the Homicide Unit during your tenure here. Only someone who has worked under the same conditions can fully comprehend the personal sacrifices that you have made in order to do your job. Not only is the work physically demanding, with long hours, little sleep, and sudden callbacks, but it also exerts an emotional toll on both the detectives and their families. Countless hours are wrenched away from spouses or partners, children and grandchildren, friends and extended family, and these are never to be recovered.

The guilt and separation begin to consume you as the mental stress from unending pressure and frustration begin to grow – (sic) a frustration that comes from having open, unsolved cases. Although your mind understands that some cases will never be solved, your heart suffers because you want each crime solved, (sic) and you hold these cases as a personal defeat. You joined this unit because you have a keen sense of right and wrong and you don't want the murderer or the evil he represents to be the victor. With experience and wisdom comes the hard realization that some things are simply beyond our control and that you have done your best when all the leads have been investigated and hope is exhausted. Even more damaging is the frustration that comes from the victim's own families, who intentionally withhold information, and from witnesses that won't admit what they saw. All too often, it seems that only the detective working the case cares about the victim. The frustration mounts as families hound you to make an arrest when you have no suspects. They complain to the media, elected officials, and your command staff that you have done nothing to investigate their case when you know that you have spent countless hours of unscheduled time on the case and sacrificed for the sake of the case by missing your child's birthday party. Very few take notice of this dedication and the personal sacrifices that you and your family have made. Little support comes from within your own organization.

For the rest of your life, you will carry the images of the horrors you have seen – (sic) visions that you can never get out of your mind. Throughout your career in Homicide, you have shared people's darkest secrets and been witness to unspeakable sins that lie hidden in the recesses of their festering souls. This also takes its toll but if you are able to step back, you know that you are dealing with society's worst and that they are a minority. What brings you back from the brink of this abyss is the knowledge that the great majority of people are decent and caring and the life that was lost so senselessly is what your efforts are fighting for.

Throughout it all, you stayed the course because you were committed to the work and what it represented. It got into your blood and became a part of your very being. The satisfaction came from cases that came together and allowed you to confront the killer - face to face – (sic) and tell him that he didn't get away with murder. The gratitude expressed by a family whose son's killer was convicted because of your efforts was the salve to the battle wounds you endured and it made all the difference. A few kind words were all you had to get back on your feet and wage the war once more.

Many sacrifices, few rewards – (sic)this is the work we have chosen. It has been a privilege to have had the opportunity to have you on my squad. I thank you."

For a Twenty, She'll Forgive Anybody

Michelle Johnson wrote the following letters and sent them to her sisters after her arrest for Erica's murder. The letters are exactly as written, including her attempts at spelling. All errors, grammatical as well as spelling, in the original are hers and not the author's errors. The first of these letters was written after she learned that Thurman McIntosh had claimed the reward money that the Move-Up Organization in Kansas City had posted as the reward. This money was a combination of dollars from many sources, including the Federal Bureau of Investigation. McIntosh knew all along about Erica's death, as did his daughter, Harrell's mother, and sundry other family members. Nevertheless, he had claimed the reward money and was now the beneficiary of Erica's blood money—the Precious Dough.

Ironically, even after writing these letters claiming to be wronged, she continued to write to Harrell and even sent him stamps so he could correspond with her. Note that all grammatical and spelling errors are from the original documents, not the author's errors.

Letter Number 1
Monday 6/6/05
Dear Stephanie,

Hello little sister How are you I hope and pray you are bless and in good health How my newphew doing T-man Could you send me some pictures of the family I miss everyone so much Did you take picture of Jasmine graduation Could you please send me some pictures of my children I miss them so much Thank you for the $30.00 that sure was a blessing to me what amazing is I fast all day Sunday for 26 hours the only think I drunk was water I read my bible God material I pray I pray for God to help me recived money I need help so bad and God knew. God sent my sister you to help me that touch my heart deeply. Sis you know what I rembered the most is when you told me to ask God to help me love myself. I do this every night, let me tell you something today 6/6/05 I seen it on the news that Pete grandpa go the reward money off my daughter. I was angry, hurt, mad, 14 thousand dollars off my baby that your own grandson kill my baby. He know for 3 ½ years. I told Pete grandpa 3 ½ years ago so he's spending blood money my daughter as that Erica. They the Move Up gave it to Pete grandpa today. I even had

01-040862

Page two

Hate cause the don't even help me in here but you collecting my baby money for what your grandson did. Sis it hurt real bad but I know I can't hate and served God. I can't judge and served God. I remberd Little Sis when you told me that Pete family couldn't care about me or Erica. If they did care they would of took me to the police station. I see and feel what you are saying. I ask myself why did I let this nigga do this to my baby. Why didn't I protect her, why Steaphanie. I am hurting so bad right now I know I need God so bad cause I don't think I can go on without him. Keep my in your prayers always. I thought I forgave them. I try so hard I just can't espically when there out there collecting money on my baby. Then I think this nigga took me down with him.

I don't know when I be able to see my children again. My baby is 14 Like today is her graduation going to 9th grade. I should be there I am her moma Look sis look where I am in jail facing 2nd degree murder child neglect I don't even know when I going to see my nieces or nephew again When I am going to see my sister or brother or even my mom and dad I love all of you I am so sorry for causing you guys so much hurt & pain I understand if you never send me any money or answer any of my calls I just thank God for you sending me money & writing me a letter. Do you know

01-040862

Page three

I found out this case is going to be going on for 2 ½ years. I have to stay in this jail for two in a half years I am praying all the time just like I had to get on my knees and pray about Pete grandpa and family. There is nothing I can do I can let God handle it like on the news, Pete grandpa acting like he just fount out. I swear to God he knew for 3 ½ years then the news ask him what's he going to do with 14 thousand dollars He said help his family out. Now you honestly time me that not wrong. Who am I to judge right. It like I forgave but can not forget. Sis please pray for me Keep me in your paryers all the time. Look, I was wondering maybe in December before Christmas the whole family can come visit me the ones who wanted to come and see me. Tell dad I found out if your coming from out of town it doesn't matter how many family members comes and you guys get to come any time or any day. I just wanted you to call before you come so it can be a contact visit where I can hug all of you. I'll write the number on the last page When you come you will be allowed to visit me any time, anyday cause you guys are going from out of town. I've been praying for this Could you please bring T-man, Jasmine, Lakiya, Elisha, Casja, Vannesa. Please Tre Toast Dawnye if there dad let's them come even bring Walter I wanted everyone to know the truth so I pray and hope my family would be here in December. Steaphanie I hope you will continue to write me your words encourage me to keep my had up and move on I trust in the Lord always. When I get out of here I don't wanted to be the same Michelle. I want to be a Christan women. I wanted to be able to love myself, resist the devil, forget the past look forward to the future. Take or be a mother to my children. Sis I just found out you can call this number 816-881-4236 start Thursday 6:00 pm you can call to set up a contact visit all the way up to Friday at 9:00 pm or you can call my case manager Mike Davis and ask him could he set up a special contact visit for the family that you are coming from Illinois Please iss I need to see yall even mom & Da. Steaphanie I love you so far you have told me the truth and leading me in the right direction. Like I said I so sorry for causing you pain and the family pain. God knows I am so sorry. I swear I am. I can't look in the past I have to keep looking or working for today The prayers verse I read a lot is John chapeter 14,15 the whole chapter John Chapter 1 verse 1-23 Romans chapter 10 verse 8, 9, 10 Romans 8L31 Romans Chapter 12 verse 12-16, Romans 3:23 Isaiah 43:25, Psalm 139 read the whole chapter Psalm 118 the whole chapter Psalm 86 the whole chapter Psalm 71 the whole chapter Psalm 27 the whole chapter the last but not least Psalm 23 read the whole chapter. Sis here a little poem that I trying to learn by heart. I thought you will like. I love all of you guys with all my heart.

: Remember, to enjoy the peace, stop trying to do something about something you cannot do anything about. If you try to live in the past life will be hard. Jesus did not say he is the great "I was". If yu try to live in the future, life will be hard. Jesus did not say he is the great "I will be". If you take each day as it comes, life will work out all right. Jesus said "I am" (John 8:58). God is always with you in each situation that is at hand. Just remember to truck in him for enough grace for today.

I hope you like this Sis. It help me out a lot in here to keep on moving with my head up high and Jesus is guiding my life. There anthor poem or prayer in the next page.

Love your sister
Michelle
PS W/B/S
I love you also thank you for the money. Keep me in your paryers always Sis

#01-040862
Page 6
I also read that verse you sent me Corinthians 13-4-8 it good. I love you Sis I still need help Keep me in my prayers also pray that God help send someone to help me with a little money. I thank you cause I bought stamps and the rest on persona Hyeine but I just couldn't get them all but I still bless that I recived that. I will call you at 5:30 pm when I come out for my hour on 6/21/05 to let you know what going on in court or what happen.
I love you Little Sis, your big sis, Michelle
God bless you & the family is always in my prayers & thoughts

#01-040862
"Five Finger Prayer"
• When you fold your hands, the thumb is nearest you. So begin by praying for those closest to you, your loved ones (Philippians 1:35)

- *The index finger is the pointer. Pray for those who teach – bible teachers and preachers, and those who teach children. (1st Thessalonians 5:25)*
- *The next finger is the tallest. It reminds you to pray for those in authority over you – national and local leaders and your supervisor at work. (1st Timothy 2:1-2)*

- *The fourth finger is usually the weakest. Pray for those who are in trouble or who are suffering (James 5:13-16)*
- *Then comes your little finger. It reminds you of your smallness in realation to God's greatness, ask him to supply your needs (Philippians 4:6, 19)*

Whatever method you use, just talk with your father. He wants to hear what's on your heart.

Over.......

#01-040862

Our prayers ascend to heavens throne
Regardless of the form we use:
Our father always hears his own
Regardless of the words we choose.
It's not the words we pray that matter
It's the condition of our heart.

Steaphanie, I hope you like these poems. It has help me in my jourey with Jesus. I hope these poems touch you like it has help me. God bless you. Keep your sister in prayers. Also pray that God send someone to help me in the money part. All I need is $25.00 to get the rest of my hyeine products. I will be straight at least for 3 months. As our sister Patricia, Daddie, Momie, anybody in our family tell them I won't bother them until 3 or 4 m.

Letter Number 2
Page 1 #01-040862
9/5/05
Monday

Love U God Bless you & family Love U Happy Labor Day!!!

Hi. How are you I hope and pray you are all right as for your sister I am so bless to have a forgiven God I am bless just serving the lord and finally loving myself I don't even know how to start this letter but I know the holy spirit will guide me to write the truth and how I feel frist let me said sorry for causing everybody so much pain & hurt I can't change the past all I can do is lear from this and do better for the future. In your letter to me you wrote you don't understand how I can let a man put me threw so much frist let me answer this question for you Frist thing I didn't love myself, I didn't know how to love anybody. Se when I was a little girl I was rape by not one not two but three people Ralph, Jody husband mom sister, then Bill you rembered the one close to Jody and Ralph then Gray dad brother I am talking about rape bad you know Gray use to pe-pe in my mouth crazy things then us as chidren not living normal lives I always felt I was the black sheep of the family. I never felt I got attention at home so I got with Larry looking for love and then when I felt I wasn't love I'll thought paying him to love me was right so I would start paying to be love then I thought you (over)

Page 2 #01-040862

had to stay by that man no matter what cause he love me yeah was I wrong. I couldn't love myself so how could I ever love anybody. Sara with the help fo the Lord I let go of my past I ask God forgiveness I had to go deep down in my soul I had a lot of things that devil thought he was holding over my head but now your sister is free, free to love Sara. I have so much peace now. Peace I never felt before in my whole life. I let my pass go I forgive everyone even Ralph, Gray, Bill for all the pain and hurt they cause me God says to forgive those who hurt you like God forgive you. So I forgive them I don't even think about the pass no more I can't change the pass I can change the future or today. You right I did make a mistake but all that time I thought it was right. I had to tell someone so yes I did tell his grandpa and mom it was driving me insane to hold that in me espically as my baby mother so I thought at the time it was right I never thought in a million years they would of took the money off my child. I don't hate nobody Sara cause I can't hate and be a child of God. At frist in my mind I hate so many people. Pete, his grandpa, his mom but I have to forgive. God will take care of them when you read that letter that got mix up the devil still had a hold on me I need money so I was telly them what they want to hear so I could get some money at that time. I was feeling their getting money off my baby I should get some too

Page 3 #01-040862
Of the money but I didn't and that's okay with me today cause God says Mark Chapter 11 verse 22-26 "Have faith in God" Jesus said what I'm about to tell you is true suppose one of you says to this mountain, "Go and throw yourself into the sea". You must not doubt in your heart. You must believe that what you say will happen. Then it will be done for you. So I tell you, when you pray for something, believe that you have already it then it will be yours, and when you start praying, forgive anyone you have anything against. Then your father in heaven will forgive your sins. Gods tell us to love our enemies. I am so tried of going the devil way of doing the devil things it time for me to have God my life. I have nothing but peace. In Matthew Chapter 7 verse 1-2 says Do not judge others. Then you will not be judged. You will be judge in the same way you judge others. You will be measured in the same way you measure others. So who am I to judge. God lets me know there no sin better than the other We all sin. I can't judge anybody. Little Sis I have to forgive and pray Do you know what's the two most important commadents in the bible love God with all your heart and soul. 2nd love you neighbors like you love yourself. You know what my problem was living in regrets of yesterday We all make mistakes there no perfect soul on this earth We all are sinner that why God send his only begotten son Jesus Christ to die for our sin. Rather than me losing my

peace over something I have done but cannot do anything about now I should

Page 4 #01-040862

trust God to make it work out all right God has the capability nobody but God, God can clean up our mistakes. So know all I try to do is enjoy peace and stop trying to do something about something I cannot do anything about If I try to live in the past, life will be hard. Jesus did not say he is the great "I was" If I try to live in the future, life will be hard Jesus did not say he is the great "I will be" If I take each day as it comes, life will work out all right Jesus said "I am". I know God is always with me in each situation that is at hand. I just have to remember to trust God for enough grace for today when I start worried Sara I just stop worrying and give God the situation. There not a day goes by that I don't think of Erica or the rest of my children but I know deep in my soul that C.J. gots my baby wrap in his arms taking care of her until I come I know my parents are taking care of Jasmine, Lakiya, Elisha. I know God is protecting all my children I pray every night for my family I don't blame my or our parents They raise all 6 of us the best they could I use to hate Ralph, Bill, Gray for taking my childhood and my family but not no more I love them cause their my brother and sister in Christ. I miss our guys so much I swear to God I do You are always on my mind and in my heart. I wish the family would find it in their heart to forgive me

Page 5 #01-040862

God knows I am truly sorry I wish I could change the hands of time but I can't I feel so good to be a new Godly person I have nothing put peace and love. I haven't heard from anyone in the family but God knows you all been in my prayers. I am not going to lie. I am hurting up here I don't recived money from anybody but as long as I serve God

I know sooner or later God will bless me with a miracle. Could you please if you can send me some pictures of the family. I need and love you guys with all my heart and soul How Jasmine, Lakiya, Elisha doing How's my niece and nephew. Kiss them all and tell them I love and miss them with all my heart and soul. Baby Sis you mean the world to me I hope and pray you can find it in your heart to forgive me. If you can't that's alright You are still my sister and I would always love you. God bless and take care of you and my niece and nephew tell K.T. and everybody I said hi I miss and love them Could you also let mom know I sign Jasmine, Lakiya, Elisha to the angel tree here in this jail so they would get in touch with her or Steaphanie I didn't know if you have the same phone number as before but I put mom work # XXX-XXX-XXXX and I put Steaphanie #XXX-XXX-XXXX cause I don't know

Page 6 #01-040862

If mom #number the same. I use (address removed) I hope they still live there I will be praying they do. Have you heard Illinois is putting charges on me too food stamp forged so they have a warrant on my too for claiming Erica on my stamps I am all right I don't worried cause the battle not mine but God All I need to do is God's will and God will fight the battle for me. I wish you could see your new Godly sister you could tell I've changed for the good. I love myself Michelle Marie Pierce Johnson. I am sending you this prayer I read every morning. I hope you read it too! I go back to court 11/10/05 Sara, please on God help your sister I need your help bad God knows I do. If you do send me money I wish you do but not I can understand too but if you do it has to be a post office money order only okay! I hope and pray to hear from you soon please in the name of Jesus send me picture of everybody in the family. You and the family would always be in my thought and prayers God Bless Kiss my baby for me. Also there a letter in here for

Casja I love you guys!! Please keep me in your thoughts and prayers. You will always be in mines. I love and miss you so much. Love, your sister Michelle

W/B/N

#01-040862 Love you "Sara Pierce"
9/5/05

"My Daily Prayer"

Please take a moment to relax your mind and humble your heart to focus on Christ. Allow God to be the only person on your mind while you read this prayer. Friends that pray together, stay together.

Dear Lord, I thank you for this day. I thank you for my being able to see and to hear this morning. I'm blessed because you are a forgiving God and an understanding God. You have done so much for me and you keep on blessing me. Forgive me this day for everything I have done, said or thought that was not pleasing to you. I ask now for your forgiveness. Please keep me safe from all danger and harm. Help me to start this day with a new attitude and plenty of gratitude. Let me make the best of each and every day to clear my mind so that I can hear from you. Please broaden my mind that I can accept all things. Let me not whine and whimper over things I have no control over. Let me continue to see sin through God's eyes and acknowledge it as evil. And when I sin, let me repent, and confess with my mouth my wrongdoing, and recive the forgiveness of God. And when this world closes in on me,

#01-040862

let me remember Jesus' example to slip away and find a quiet place to pray. It's the best response when I am pushed beyond my limits. I know that when I can't pray, you listen to my heart. Continue to use me to do your will. Continue to bless me that I may be a blessing to others. Keep me uplifted that I hay have words of encouragement for others. I pray for those that are lost and can't find their way. I pray for all those that are misjudged and misunderstood. I prya for those who don't know you intimately. I pray for those that don't belive. But I thank you that I believe. I believe that God changes people and God changes things. I pray for all my sisters and brothers, and for each and every family member in their households. I pray for peace, love and joy in their homes that they are out of debt and all their needs are meet. I pray that every eye that reads this knows there is no problem, circumstance or situation greater than God. Every battle is in your hands for you to fight. I pray that these words be received in the hearts of every eye that sees them and every mouth that confesses them willingly.

This is my prayer in Jesus's name, "Amen"

Page 7 #01-040862

P.S. I have a picture of Erica a big one would you like one if you do let me know all I have to do is buy a big envelope off canteen when God bless me with money I can send it to you I have 4 of the same pictures big one of her so let me know if you would like one of your niece! Bless you Sis !!!

Letter Number 3

Page 1 #01-040862

Dear Little Sis Stephanie,

Hello how are you doing As for your sister I am bless taking day for day living for God and doing God will not mine. I am glad to hear you are doing okay. I haven't wrote because I wrote Sara and I haven't heard anything back from her. I wrote you last and didn't hear from you I've been writing Jasmine, Lakiya, Elisha haven't recived no letters from them Wrote mom & dad ask for pictures of the family Haven't received nothing so I didn't know if anybody still stay in Huntington or if anybody even want me to write then You know something sister I know I made lots of bad choices in my life hurt losts of people espically my children & family All I can do is ask for forgiveness for all my pain & hurt I cause everyone. I can't dwell on the past or my regrets that's what the devil wants me to do Loose my peace and joy I can't change the past all I can do is live for today try my hardest to change me for the good of God I had lots of trouble forgiving myself if I couldn't forgive myself, how did I expect God to forgive me. I had to learn to forgive Michelle and love

P.S. I go back to court 11/10/05 I don't worried cause this battle not mines but God I let go and let God Love you, Sis

Page 2 #01-040862

Michelle. I learning to do this everyday I learning I don't need a man to love me as long as I have the love of our father Jesus Christ. I've been looking for love in all the wrong places all this time all I need was Jesus Christ love When you have that love you don't need any other The two most important commdants is love the lord our God with all your heart and soul and the 2nd one is love your neighbor as you love yourself. You know your words of encouragement is what help me to who I am today a child of God. I don't want to be the same Michelle as I came in here as Sis. I want and is a new creature in Jesus Christ Old things are pass away I became a new creature in God. You know I cry when I read in my bible how they people crucify Jesus, spit on him, beat him put nails in his hands a crown over his head until he bleed. I don't want to be like those people who just sat there and watch Jesus or laugh at Jesus. I want to fell Jesus pain. I want to serve God Jesus didn't have to die for our sin but he love us sinners so much he did. All I do everyday is sit in this jail is God will not Michelle but God I am glad I am here in jail

Page 3 #01-040862

I know you wondering why did I said this I said it because I am not where I want to be but thank God I not where I used to be. I learn a lot about myself, and our Lord Jesus Christ. I let the past go know. I living for God day by day. Amen. I am sending you this prayer in this letter. I hope it helps you as it has help me. If you don't mind could you please send me some pictures of everybody and write and let me know how everybody doing. If it's no trouble could you also send me some money If not I understand I put my faith and trust in Jesus. If I continue to seek the kingdom of God our Father would supply my needs. I've been praying for God to help me money wise now it's my part to pray, believe and keep faith that it would happen. I happy to hear you think about me That touch my heart and soul in a major way I know you love me I love you I've been praying to God all the time even fasting to hear from someone in my family and God answer my prayers you wrote me. I've always have you and the family on my mind and prayers always. I hope to God you and me do keep in touch more. I would love that a lot Sis. So Elisha wants to play basketball. I glad to hear that Stephanie I can't wait until I be a part of my children life I

Page 4 #01-040862

Know I miss so much of their lives but my prayers is asking God for one more chance to be their mother, a Godly mother. I know I have a lot to show everybody and prove but as long as I have Jesus in my life we can do this together as one with each other. I know the devil will try all things but I stay fast with the Lord Jesus Christ. So Jasime and Nikki is doing good in school I so proud of them So T-man and Elisha is anthor story, huh I have all you guys in my prayers

I hope to see some kind of family during the holiday if not, I still would have my one and only family in my prayer. Please in the name of Jesus help me out with some money anything will help beggar can't be pickey. God knows I can't be anyway. Tell mom and dad everybody I said I'm sorry for all the pain and hurt I cause the family to please forgive me God bless and take care. Can't wait to hear from you again.

God bless you all
Love you Sis

Michelle PS Read the prayer every day God bless you

#01-040862
"My Daily Prayer"

Please take a moment to relax your mind and humble your heart to focus on Christ. Allow God to be the only person on your mind while you read this prayer. Friends that pray together, stay together.

Dear Lord, I thank you for this day. I thank you for my being able to see and to hear this morning. I'm blessed because you are a forgiving God and an understanding God. You have done so much for me and you keep on blessing me. Forgive me this day for everything I have done, said or thought that was not pleasing to you. I ask now for your forgiveness. Please keep me safe from all danger and harm. Help me to start this day with a new attitude and plenty of gratitude. Let me make the best of each and every day to clear my mind so that I can hear from you. Please broaden my mind that I can accept all things. Let me not whine and whimper over things I have no control over. Let me continue to see sin through God's eyes and acknowledge it as evil. And when I sin, let me repent, and confess with my mouth my wrongdoing, and recive the forgiveness of God. And when this world closes in on me, Page One let me remember Jesus' example to slip away and find a quiet place to pray. It's the best response when I am pushed beyond my limits. I know that when I can't pray, you listen to my heart. Continue to use me to do your will. Continue to bless me that I may be a blessing to others. Keep me uplifted that I hay have words of encouragement for others. I pray for those that are lost and can't find their way. I pray for all those that are misjudged and misunderstood. I prya for those who don't know you intimately. I pray for those that don't belive. But I thank you that I believe. I believe that God changes people and God changes things. I pray for all my sisters and brothers, and for each and every family member in their households. I pray for peace, love and joy in their homes that they are out of debt and all their needs are meet. I pray that every eye that reads this knows there is no problem, circumstance or situation greater than God. Every battle is in your hands for you to fight. I pray that these words be received in the hearts of every eye that sees them and every mouth that confesses them willingly.

This is my prayer in Jesus's name, "Amen"

#01-040862
God Bless You!!! Sis I ♥U

Can I Get A Witness?

It didn't take long for Michelle Johnson to find religion in prison. She didn't stand a chance from the day she was born; however, many of us rise above physical and sexual abuse and lead productive lives. She elected to take the low road by marrying Harrell after Erica's death and having two more children with him. It's that Bill Cosby joke about "making another one that looks just like you," only it's not funny—it's a travesty. They used the welfare system like a product line for their own cottage industry—they produced babies and made money at it. They didn't keep any of them. They were either given away or, as in Erica's case, taken from a loving home, beaten, sexually assaulted, murdered, decapitated, and thrown away. Michelle continued to list Erica on the welfare rolls and collect assistance in her name for years after the child's death. She had five children with her first husband, and her mother raised the first three girls. Larry Green's mother had the little boy until her health prevented her from keeping him. He was sent to foster care. Being voluntarily surrendered to Family Services must have a tremendously negative impact on an individual, laying the groundwork for a sense of abandonment and fostering the feelings of rejection that bring about behaviors that lead to drugs, crime, and detachment. The last child with her first husband ended up dead in a trash pile. By the time she met

Harrell Johnson, she was reasonably astute at discarding babies in one manner or another.

Sonnets from the Slammer

Michelle wasn't the only one writing letters. Harrell wrote love letters to his darling Michelle, the likes of which would have the poet Robert Browning rolling in his grave. While Browning wrote of showering leaves caressing his beloved Elizabeth Barrett, good ol' Harrell wrote of golden showers. Honestly. Of particular interest was one dated August 3, 2007, 6:04 p.m., which reads as follows (all errors, grammatical as well as spelling, in the original, are his and not the author's errors):

Mrs. Johnson,

What's up with my one and only wife? I pray all is well your way. As for me I'm content. Just wishin we were together with our kids. Trust & believe our day is coming. Well I just got a letter from you #3. So my day is going to be a nice day. So you got that money I see. Maybe if you have it I need for you to send me 8 single stamps cause I owe Richard Davis a bag of cheese popcorn he got for me today. I can pay him in stamps. So if you can send me any stamps I can use them. Well let me get to your letter to me. Man this letter is smelling so good. Is that how you smellin down there? I can't wait to hold you in my arms. Oh yeah before I forget. I tried to call Rhonda at the day-care earlier and the phone was disconnected. I tried the other day-care number and it wasn't on either. And I had my case manager call information and they said they didn't have no kids world day-care in Muskogee so I don't know what's up. They might have closed down the day-care. I called the house phone 918-XXX-XXXXand no one answered the phone. Ain't nobody wrote and told me nothing. I pray they all alright there. Your husband is blessed up here. Just missing you and our kids so much. I wish you could come lay with me. I'll hold you so tight and never let go. We want to make love to you two to! I love you to baby. Yeah I was hurting on our babies birthday too. She 7 years old. It hurts so much we can't be there for them right now. I know they need us. I cry a lot cause we don't even know how our kids even look, that really eat's me up. So we got to fight these people for our life and freedom back as long as we stay together as one and don't take no deal we'll beat this case and they know it my love. I really need you to get rid of that lwyer as soon as possible. he's the problem, Michelle. If you was to go home to our kids you'll get on that now. cause he trying to sell you out. Please understand that my love. he's not for us at all.

Page 2

Yeah I will never forget the time you gave birth to ~~my~~ our big girl. That was the best day of my life. I cried ~~stay~~ standing there watching you push piggie out. I did hold your leg open that nurse told me to and when she come out my first words was it's a boy and the nurse said no it's a girl. I just let those tears go. Michelle we go to do what we got to do together as one. Whatever it takes to get home to our kids and families. We don't owe no body up here in Kansas City shit. We take what happen to God and old God. We can beat this case and that's real talk. You just go to do everything I ask you to do and listen to me. They violated our rights in so many ways your lawyer knows this, but he not trying to help you bring it out. So you got to fire his ass now. That's why I told you to spint in his face cause it'll be easyer for you and if you do it real good he'll get off yo' case his~~elf~~

self. Yes. Please do exactly what you said your going to do to that lawyer in this letter. And tell him right after you spit in his face tell him you going to keep doing that until he get off your case. Please do it my love. Boo if they don't have the evidence then they can't get no conviction at all. That's why they keep coming at you with all its is is in those pleas. Cause they know you go to trial you'll beat the case they know it. You got to put two and two together. Then you'll see what they are trying to do. And that's why I tell you to tell me everything that lawyer say to you and do so I'll know what he up to. We got to see them coming or see what they trying to do so we can go another route feel me? So you got to communicate with me about everything they do in your case when you get in fornt of the judge tell him everything that what that lawyer ain't doing, get yourself on record okay. Boo I know you can

Page 3

do it. Michelle on the real that punk ass layer to be spit in his face. He need his ass whipped for real. Cause he playing with our life and freedom. When he knows the case is weak. Boo look they all even my lawyers would sell us out when they know these white people violated our rights. They will help their own kind before they help us, so we got to stay on they ass and make them do their job. Boo they going to try and slide shit up under us. But as long as we stay focus and stay on these people we'll be cool. I need you to help me my love. Tell your judge you' ve asked that lawyer to file a motion for a change of venue and he won't. Boo keep calling that lawyer until he comes up here and you do what you got to do okay. Boo you got to take matters into your own hands at times. So god'll understand what you did was best. Yeah I sit in here and remaicse about the past too. How we both use to wash each other's back and bodies. I miss us doing all that too. Do you remember us giving each other golden shower? What about us peeing in each other's mouth? We used to do a lot of crazy, freakie things in our apartment huh? Yes I'm on a low sodium diet and I think the reason why I coughed up that blood was because of my allergices I'm taking a benhydrill pill for that now. Yeah we on this same kind of tray all I get is firut too on all my trays expect breakfast. My love you are the only woman for me. Hey when you get my letters let me know you got it by telling me the number # of the letter okay. That way I'll know which letter you got. I need you in my life too Mrs. Michelle Marie Johnson. I love my new radio. I be beating hard up here. Thanks boo! Boo I told you in my last letter what I did with those stamps. I sent that lawyer in Oklahoma City a copy of everything I ~~felled~~ filed to the federal court in Muskogee against Muskogee and Wagoner and I sent it all certified

Page 4

Mail which costed over $5.07 cause I sent him over 20 something pages so that's where those stamps went and I write you with one of them on that card I sent to you I believe it was. My love when you send me stamps I used them to write you unless it's important I'll use them on something else. Look I got to give Richard Davis 6 single stamps for this bag of cheese popcorn he bought for me so please send me 8 single stamps if you got it. I told him I was writing you and getting them from you by next week. The reason why I said send me 8 single stamps is because I don't have any and that money was on my books so long I couldn't order a indigent pack. Check game about/ Mike-mike (Micheal Brown). Look all you need to remember is this and this is all you need to know. Anybody ask you any other questions you tell them to ask me. ~~I (me) walked to the store to get some cigarettes~~ we was already talking about taking Erica back to Oklahoma once we got the check on the first. Because we couldn't keep no food in that house. Whommes (sp) kids and her was eating up everything and it just stayed drity in that house and nasty. So we decided we *was going to take Erica back as soon as we got the check on the 1st. So one day I (me) walked to the store to get some cigarettes and I ran into Mike-mike. We talked a few and he told me he was heading back to Oklahoma. I told him we'll give him $35.00 dollars. We drove back to the house on 59th and the rest xxxxxxxxxxxx read is all you know. Start here are all you know. I came into the house and told you that Mike-mike would take Erica back to Oklahoma for $35.00 dollars. We packed her things you wrote down the address and phone number to betty's house's. We took Eric out to the car and said our goodbyes I gave him M.M. the address and phone with the money. We kissed our baby bye and we watch them leave. Now Mike-mike had his daughter sara with him he told us he was up there are to get her and take*

Page 5

Her back to Oklahoma she was about 9 or 8 years old brown skinned short hair. You knew Mike-mike through me and Muskogee cause he worked on two of my cars before you M.J. remember him putting the motor in the grey chevy. That's how you know him. Seen him a few times around the hood. The next day Mike-mike called us in the evening and said he'd dropped the baby off. So you called right after he hung up and talked to one of the foster kids there and they said yes Eric Kidd did get dropped off she was gone to the store with betty. That's all you were told. We had already xxxx said we were going to take Erica back to Oklahoma on the 1st when we got the check because the living conditions was foul on 59th and we couldn't keep no food in the house for us to eat and it was always drity. People in and out. So I (me) told you we could save a lot of money if we send Erica back by M-m for $35.00 dollars. We felt she would be safe. Boo that's all you know don't answer any questions you don't know send them to me. Look that's just something you need to keep in mind cause this is our way to the town. Say I'm going to write it out for you the whole thing but you only *need to remember the parts that's pertaining to you okay/do list best and don't show no one. Please I'll always think of you when I listen to my Sony radio. I'll never sell it never that. I wish I could be in your sports bra right now! We can listen to the radio at the same time but I like listening to 107.3 after 10:00 pm cause they always playing slow jams. So tell me is that monday & wed or monday thru wed? I like a lot of those songs my favorite is the new Marah carey love with Bon thugs & Bow wow. T.i new one. T-Pain-Shawanty. And that white boy Robin Thickes old song I forgot the name of that one. but I got a lot of those songs I like. You need to write out the times we can listen to the radio's together. I want you to start listening to 107.3 with me at night so check monday thru friday at 11:00 pm to 12:00 am and we can listen to cool wange 90.1 at 12:00 am.*

**I walked to a store, Countryview to buy cigarettes. While there I came acres i.e. ran into a guy I know as Mike-Mike (real name Micheal Brown). We talked for a few about what was happening. Mike-Mike had his daughter with him. He said he was heading back to Oklahoma. Then I ask if we would do me a favor, since he (Mike-Mike) was going up there, if he be willing to take y stepdaughter Eric back with him, since he was taking his daughter Sara to drop her off, that I'd be willing to pay him #35.00 for expenses. He agreed and we rode back to the house where my wife and kids were at. Once there, yo part to remember from here on out, I went inside to get my wife and baby i.e. (Erica) you had Piggie. The 4 of us came out together. I opened the back door of the car to put Erica in. Then I got back in the front seat to pay Mike-Mike, while my wife stood on the curb. I told my wife to let me speak to Mike-Mike and she, my wife, gave me the information on where to take E, once Mike-Mike got to Muskogee and the phone number to the house so he could call once he drop E off. We talked for about ½ hour before he left. Before E left, my wife gave the baby a kiss & hug, so did I. The I closed the car door to talk* *a minute, you know, to kinda catch up on whats happening. Basically that's it, other than we watch them leave going west on 59th street. Tht was the last time we saw or heard from E, Mike-Mike and his daughter Sara. He did call the next day in the evening saying he'd dropped the baby off. I related the information to my wife and she called betty to make sure E had been dropped off safely. She talked to one of the foster kids to her knowledge that's who she talked to. And she was told E did make it there safe and that she was out with betty. So we felt everthing was alright. About 2 weeks later we heard bits and pieces about a bab was killed in Kansas city, it was all over the news. We had no reason to think we were connected to the case!! This is our defence. We sent her back. Baby they got to know we we dunit and they can't just study it and the other part I wrote for you this is what I wrote for myself and what I told the lawyers. All you remember was that the car was gray and 4-door. You don't know what kid of car it was.*

Questions to remember...

#1. Don't answer any questions about exact time and dates. Because you cannot be for sure. Since it has been years gone by.

#2 Repeat, if asked, exactly above statement and (#1) about time & dates.

#3. Do not attempt to answer any questions nor guess at them, if you cannot be for sure – just say; I'm not for sure or I don't know.

#4 Again! Erica's keeper betty came to my wife's job Mcdonalds so we thought everthins was okay.

#5 stay insteide the frame work of your statement above to everone who ask. It must be the same, short, direct and to the point.

#6 Take your time and think before answering any questions. And don't be in a rush, take your time.

All the above is what was written up for me
This is my statement, I wrote what you need to remember and only that.
Please me know when you get this.

I love that T-Pain & Watt could, Shawty

Cool wayne come on at 12:00 am every friday morning.

I always listen to cool wayne every Friday morning. And you can pick the time to listen to 1590 am. I be checking it out sometimes I got it locked in the radio so tell me the times. I see how you looked out for me on the radio. Thank you. I love you with all my heart and soul. I won't mess with this radio at all it don't need no fixing at all like that old piece of shit I had. No I ain't heard from Adrian in a while like 5,6 months. They sent my letters back to me about 3 months ago. So I ain't wrote back. Try to write him okay. I'm on my laywers to gonna have to wait till we file this motion to the courts on October 18th cause your lawyer is holding our visit up. I apologize to you about that picture. I'm over that my love. Canit nothing, I mean nothing, come between our love we have for one another or our marriage. I can't wait to get my ass whipping I miss us making love to my love. Yeah I remember I ate my pussy at night and morning in Chi town. That's was a nice night. You was nutting in my mouth so much. I really miss eating cookie. I love when you made me eat cookie. I'm about to come out for my hour in a little bit. It's 9:00 and I got to was you body oh yeah and we was smoking well I was smoking that shit all night in sara's basement. You really had to clown suit on that talk about how you was getting that dudes money. Do you remember all that when I read the part where you said you played with cookie in the shower and nutted to. Panthon got so damn hard, he miss you and his pussy cookie. When we take a shower tonight we going to bust a nut thinking about you and cookie. You got me horny fo' real I want to fuck you so bad my love. Yeah, I figured they'll put that female in there with you all who tried to cut that baby out that girl. But do you see how they keep coming at you with those please that should tell you they ain't got no case against you. Fuck a plea we goin' to trial okay? You better tell them hoes you in love with this dic fo' real You mines for life and I'm yours. Well let me go take a shower. It's my hour out 9:17 pm. Hey do they let you keep your T.V. on at night after 10:00 pm on weekdays? Ours be on all night. I'm back. Your bod is so, so clean. My love please let me know when you get this letter. Well baby I'm going to end this for now. I'll write you again soon. I got to write out this paper for you. Boo just remember the parts I wrote in this letter. I'll let you know when we might have to tell it to your new lawyer. I've already told it to my new lawyers. When we talk face to face I'll put you up on it clearly. If you have any questions please asked me don't be so wide open with it. Okay I love you so much.

Your husband
Harrell laron Johnson Sr.

I (heart) U
moma cee

The next time we fast
you pick the date and what
two meals we ain't going
to eat okay my love

W/B/N

S/W/A/K

My Sister's Keeper

On February 20, 2006, Michelle Johnson's mother gave statements to police during an audiotaped interview at her home in Aurora, Illinois. She confirmed that she was Johnson's mother and that Johnson's biological father was named Lee Pierce. In addition, she provided details about Michelle's background, her children by Larry Green and Harrell Johnson, and her contacts with Michelle both before and after the child's body was discovered. She also provided a copy of the court document that gave her custody of Michelle's three oldest children by Larry Green.

During that same month, Johnson's biological sister, Stephanie Pierce, provided a videotaped statement to police that Michelle had called her from jail after her arrest and told her what had happened to Erica. Upon questioning, Pierce also stated that Michelle had told Harrell's mother what happened to Erica just a few months after Erica's murder. She further noted that Michelle was afraid of being arrested if she tried to get help for the child, as Michelle had outstanding warrants. Harrell threatened to tell the police about the warrants if she were to try and get medical help for Erica. These details once again corroborated statements that Michelle was more afraid of going to jail than she was that her child was dying.

Another of Michelle's sisters, Sara Pierce, was also interviewed by police. During a videotaped account, she provided the names of Michelle's children with Larry Green. She confirmed that her mother, Barbara Farence, gained custody of two girls when DFS took the children after their father threw an ashtray, striking both Michelle and one of the children in the face. When she was born, the third baby was given to Barbara because she "was a crack baby." Sara further related that the first time she saw Erica, Michelle was involved with a man named Jonathan Clemmons in 1998 (her husband's stepbrother). It was the only time she had ever seen Erica. Michelle and Harrell would come for a few months and then leave for Oklahoma. After that, it seemed to be an annual trek back and forth to stay with whoever would have them. Harrell was thrown out once for groping one of Michelle's nieces—her sister Patricia's daughter—and Sara finally had enough when Harrell charged $1,000 in Western Union charges on her credit card.

Pierce further stated that she received a phone call from Thurman McIntosh, Harrell's grandfather—two days before the arrest for Erica's murder. However, McIntosh didn't make much sense and was very difficult to understand. This same inability to understand McIntosh and his nonsensical ramblings caused call takers so much difficulty trying to make sense of his calls to the hotline.

However, she said that Michelle would later tell her that both McIntosh and Deborah Allendale knew about Erica's death a few months after it happened. They kept quiet until McIntosh decided to turn them in for the reward money, which infuriated Michelle. Sara related that when Michelle told her the events leading to Erica's death and that she didn't call for help because of her warrants, Sara asked her why didn't she drop Erica at an emergency room and then "bail" so that she didn't get arrested. But instead, Michelle just kept saying, "I know, I know."

Sara's other significant statement was to tell the detectives that Michelle had told her about officers canvassing the area after the body was found. However, she lied and said that a man was lurking around the neighborhood at roughly the same time the incident occurred. She also told Sara that she attended all the vigils held for "Precious Doe."

Sara showed courage in contacting the police and sharing what she learned. It was hard to imagine that these two women were the product of the same family. It would have changed the story's outcome if Michelle had just reached out and called Sara when Erica was injured. If the little girl had been left at a hospital, her identity still wouldn't have initially been known, but Erica Green would have lived to sing and play another day.

Tidying Up the Housekeeping Issues

On Friday, July 18, 2008, Harrell's preliminary hearing was conducted in the Jackson County Courthouse, and Harrell Johnson's trial date was set for October 6, 2008. The prosecution team consisted of Timothy Dollar, Special Assistant Prosecuting Attorney; James Kanatzar, Prosecuting Attorney; and Assistant Prosecutors Dan Miller and Dawn Parsons. The public defenders representing Harrell would be Kenton M. Hall and Christopher Slusher. This was the time for both sides to tidy up loose ends and address all the issues that needed airing out before the trial. Johnson wanted unlimited access to his attorneys and was indignant that they wouldn't accept his collect calls. Collect calls from correctional facilities are processed through a special service that costs between $10 - $15 a minute. It's prohibitive for defense attorneys to incur these, especially when the clients want to ramble on about their cases. So the Court entered an order for Johnson to have access to a phone once a week to speak with his attorneys.

Then he had a gripe about access to exercise. He claimed that he was being punished and that it was an attempt by "them" to break him down and get him to admit to something he hadn't done. He was adamant that his rights to "recreation" were being denied. The defendant withdrew a request for a change of venue, and the State submitted a proposal to waive the original appeal for the death penalty. It was a heinous crime but did not meet the criteria for a capital case in the State of Missouri. The Court approved both. Over the next two months, Harrell would be hauled back to court for more issues, and he whined about this and that. Then there was the issue of eyeglasses. It certainly was reasonable and appropriate to get him glasses so that he could see all the photos and other evidence that the Prosecution was showing to the jury. Didn't want him to miss anything. He was less than happy with the healthcare being provided to him, as the court transcripts show: Note that all grammatical and spelling errors are from the original documents, not the author's errors.

THE COURT: All right. If I may ask, Mr. Johnson, what's your vision? Can you see? Do you have distance problems or reading problems?

THE DEFENDANT: Distance problems. They checked my eyes. They supposed to take me out to Truman. The TMC was over at the jail, they got a new policy or something now, and they don't know what they're doing. I mean, they doing their own thing. They not abide by anything that was written, I guess the prescription that was written and everything.

THE COURT: Have you worn glasses in the past?

THE DEFENDANT: Yes, sir.

THE COURT: Who filled your last prescription, do you know?

THE DEFENDANT: It was in Oklahoma, back when I was a juvenile.

THE COURT: Okay. Well, I'll call over there and see if they can do something and get your eyes right.

THE DEFENDANT: I'll appreciate it.

Although the Johnsons were frequent visitors to their facilities, the public hospital's free services now apparently failed to meet the lofty expectations of a registered felon.

The Court denied the State's request to introduce evidence of sexual abuse of Erica Green, evidence of physical abuse of Erica Green that was unrelated to the cause of death, evidence of welfare fraud on the part of the defendant, and evidence that the defendant spent time in the Oklahoma Department of Corrections.

The Court upheld the request by the State to introduce the prior convictions during the penalty phase of the trial only. The Court also allowed the introduction of evidence surrounding the victim's beheading to be submitted by the State. This was an issue Harrell vehemently opposed. There was also a limitation on the media present in the courtroom during the proceedings.

The defense didn't want police officers to testify in uniform even though that appearance was within the scope of their employment. Then they didn't want the State to be able to ask witnesses if they had agreed to provide truthful testimony. This was directly related to Michelle Johnson's agreement to do precisely that as a part of her plea agreement. Although this was standard legal language, it was the defense's position that this bolstered her credibility with the jury. Finally, they also wanted to ensure the State didn't ask any witnesses about Harrell's apparent lack of remorse. But, of course, the State didn't plan on it, so it was a moot point.

The defense wanted something done preemptively about any potential family reactions or outbursts, which is generally the Court managing the issues when these occur. No such eruptions ever happened, and the agreement ended up being that witnesses would be cautioned before the testimony and that was sufficient. The defense also didn't want any photographs of Erica Green (aka "Precious Doe") shown that had been taken while she was alive. They couldn't get the evidence photos thrown out for obvious reasons, but they took their shot at trying to dehumanize the victim. Make her a corpse but don't show the living, breathing little girl who was beaten, sexually abused, killed, brutally dismembered, stripped of her clothing, and dumped like a broken doll in a wooded trash heap. "The truth shall set you free" wasn't going to play in Harrell's favor, so the defense lawyers did their best not to tell it if they could avoid it.

Compelling Testimony

On October 1, 2008, the jury for Harrell's trial was selected, and testimony began on October 6, 2008. Thomas Young, M.D., a forensic pathologist, and Gregory Hornig, a pediatric neurosurgeon, were called to testify. In addition, Police Officer Jason Russley and crime scene investigators Diane Lutman and Melissa Thompson were called to the stand, along with Danny Phillips and Sgt. Bernard.

Witness for the Prosecution

Michelle Johnson appeared before Judge John O'Malley on September 13, 2007. To avoid a first-degree murder charge, Michelle had pleaded guilty to Second Degree Felony Murder, Child Endangerment, Tampering with Evidence, and Improper Disposal of a Body in exchange for a deal of 25 years in prison if she testified truthfully against Harrell. This sentence would set a release date in 2030 but afford her a chance for parole.

On October 7, 2008, Michelle testified in court against Harrell. She acknowledged that as part of her plea agreement, she was serving 25 years in the Missouri Department of Corrections and that she also had to testify truthfully against Harrell to keep the agreed sentencing recommendation. Michelle testified that she had been sexually abused by an uncle and one of his friends and that she started using drugs at 13. She stated she was the daughter of Barbara Terence and Lee Andrew Pierce. She said she had five children by Larry Green: Jasmine Ciera Green, Lakiya Dawn Green, Elisha Josephanie Green, Larry Don Green, Jr., and Erica Michelle Marie Green. In March 1997, Michelle Johnson was convicted of retail theft again. She already had four previous felony convictions, but her sentences were suspended until the newest arrest. However, it resulted in the court revoking those suspensions, and she was now to serve two years in prison. Because she was eight months pregnant, Michelle was incarcerated at the Mabel Bassett Correctional Center in McCloud, Oklahoma, where all pregnant inmates are housed. Michelle confirmed that on May 14, 1997, she was taken by the Department of Corrections to the Oklahoma University Medical Center in Oklahoma City to deliver Erica Green and that she signed over custody of her infant to Betty Brown on May 16, 1997. Michelle stated she got out of prison in October 1997 and got Erica back from Betty Brown in November. She kept the baby for about six months but then returned her to Brown. She stated she had previously become acquainted with Harrell Johnson in 1995 when he was a customer—her john. After her prison release, she began a relationship with Harrell, and he moved in with her in 1999. Despite his having used her as a prostitute, Michelle indicated she liked how Harrell treated her, as he did not beat her like Larry Green and provided her with drugs. They subsequently moved in with Johnson's mother. They moved in and out of that home for several years until 2005.

In 2001, they moved to KC and lived with Rachelle Allendale, Johnson's cousin, at 59th and Kensington, crowded in the back bedroom with their six-month-old daughter Markeshia. They stayed there until Erica's murder, moved to Chicago until they wore out their welcome a few months later, and then headed back to Muskogee. Michelle told everyone in Chicago that Erica was with her father in Oklahoma, and she told people in Oklahoma that her mother was taking care of Erica in Illinois.

As she testified against Harrell, Michelle stated that she knew her child would die without medical assistance but that she and Harrell had outstanding warrants for their arrest. She and Harrell elected to watch the little girl slowly die a cruel and needless death over three days rather than risk going back to jail. Michelle was in the courtroom with her lover/abuser/husband/baby killer for half of the day but did not make eye contact with him until she was asked to identify the man who killed her daughter. She waved her hand in his direction at the defense table but said nothing. What was there to say?

Harrell's videotaped confession to Kansas City detectives while in custody in Muskogee, Oklahoma, was played for the jury. After this and Michelle's testimony, Harrell elected not to testify in his defense. His testimony would have been a waste of the Court's time. His lawyers had a motion for a Judgment of Acquittal at the Close of the State's Evidence and a motion to dismiss the case for lack of evidence—dismiss Murder, First Degree, charges for lack of evidence of premeditation. After the video, the jury was dismissed for the remainder of the day.

Day of Reckoning

On Wednesday, October 8, 2008, the morning court session was for closing arguments. Mr. Slusher gave the court some long diatribe about John Adams defending the British. He and Mr. Hall seemed to be reasonable gentlemen with the dubious task of defending a confessed murderer. They were the defense team, but it was hard to figure out who and what they were defending with that speech. Perhaps it was a valiant attempt to protect their status as human beings, hoping not to be tarred and feathered for defending the indefensible acts of brutality that took the life of an innocent child. Given that tarring and feathering was a customary punishment in the days of John Adams, it's not unreasonable to think that this thought may have indeed crossed their minds.

Slusher closed by asking the jury to find Harrell guilty only of Involuntary Manslaughter in the First Degree. Now it was the Prosecution's turn to give their argument.

The Verdict

The following is a copy of the transcript of Tim Dollar's powerful closing statement to the jury: Note that all grammatical and spelling errors are from the original documents and not the author's errors.

"So, with that, I have this closing thought to leave you with. What will the correct verdict, the right verdict, mean? It will mean that there will be a public and permanent record for all eternity as to what happened in this case. It will mean that 20 years from now, 30 years from now, maybe even 50 years from now, someone can make their way to the Jackson County Courthouse, maybe even little Markeshia who grows up and wants to find out what happened to her sister, and they'll be directed to some storage room in the courtroom, and it will probably be some dark and damp place, and they can -- they can ask for File Number 0516-2893, State of Missouri vs. Harrell Johnson, and maybe even someone will have written in magic marker on the front of it "Precious Doe," and they'll brush off the dust and they'll comb through the file, and they'll pull out that piece of paper, and it will be signed by your foreman, and it will say we, the jury, on Count I find the defendant, Harrell Johnson, guilty of Murder in the First Degree, and then they'll know that on October 8th, 2008, the hundreds and hundreds of hours of police work paid off, six years of community involvement

were worth it; that Kansas City's long nightmare was over; that a little three-year-old girl can rest in peace, and that finally someone, someone stood up for "little E," someone stood up for Precious Doe, someone stood up for Erica Michelle Marie Green. Thank you very much."

The jury retired to deliberate at 11:47 a.m. At 2:05 p.m., the jury requested to see either Harrell's videotaped confession with Detective Phillips or the transcript if they couldn't view the tape. Both legal teams agreed, and the judge approved it. Observers were sent back into the hall while jurors were escorted down to watch the video in the courtroom. Once that was over, the waiting game began again. By 3:15 p.m., the court was notified that a verdict had been decided. It was hard to look at the jurors and tell their collective decision.

After reviewing the documents, the judge asked Harrell to stand, and he read the following:

"As to Count I, we, the jury, find the defendant, Harrell L. Johnson, guilty of Murder in the First Degree as submitted in Instruction Number 5. Accordingly, we assess and declare the punishment for Murder in the First Degree at imprisonment for life without eligibility for probation or parole."

"As to Count II, we, the jury, find the defendant, Harrell L. Johnson, guilty of Endangering the Welfare of a Child in the First Degree as submitted in Instruction Number 13."

"As to Count III, we, the jury, find the defendant, Harrell L. Johnson, guilty of Abuse of a Child as submitted in Instruction Number 15".

The judge then instructed the jury on the procedures for determining the sentences for Counts II and III. He advised that they would hear arguments from the prosecution and the defense. These were the last issues that the jury would be deliberating.

There was no new evidence, so Kanatzer and Slusher presented final arguments. Kanatzer thanked the jury for their service and asked that they give Harrell Johnson the maximum sentence on each count.

Slusher stated that it seemed odd to say so but that he, Mr. Hall, and Harrell accepted the findings of the Court. He just wanted to mention that they did take issues with the State's position that there was no remorse in this case.

He argued that Harrell was concerned about himself, but it was possible that he, too, felt guilt for the murder. Doesn't that count for something? Didn't the jury think Harrell might feel bad for Erica even though he killed the child, cut off her head, hid the body, and lied about it for years? After all, the defense didn't argue the charges, didn't drag out the case, and nitpick every piece of evidence. Didn't that count for something? They didn't put up too much of a fight, considering the evidence mounted against Harrell. The jury had viewed his tearful confession when he met with Michelle and the detectives. Couldn't they consider that? It was incumbent upon Mr. Slusher to ask for mercy, but it was painful to watch.

The role of a defense attorney is a profession that the *Discovery* Channel will undoubtedly never feature on *Dirty Jobs.* Still, the tasks are as distasteful and ugly as Mike Rowe's undertaken on that show. By all accounts, Mr. Slusher and Mr. Hall are decent men who shared the unpleasant task of tying a fancy ribbon on a killer and trying to defend his inhumane treatment of a defenseless little girl.

The judge instructed the jury on the verdict forms and next steps, and by 4:09 p.m., they began to deliberate, so the court was in recess once again. In a piece of irony, the word "recess" conjures the notion that you go to the playground and play on the swing. It brought to mind the swing set in the park where Erica's makeshift memorial was created, just yards from where her discarded body was found.

At 6:09 p.m. the jury had a question. *"How many years term does a life sentence carry?"* It was a puzzling question, and Hall, Kanatzer, and the judge agreed that the judge couldn't answer the specific question as it was an indeterminate sentence based on how long the individual might live and that they needed to use the jury instructions as a guide. That took one minute, and we were back on the see-saw until 6:44 p.m. when the jury indicated they had trouble arriving at a unanimous decision regarding Count III, the child abuse charge. At that point, the public defender promptly requested a mistrial, for which he was swiftly told "no."

This time when the jury returned, the judge read additional instructions, and they went back to deliberate one more time. It was 6:51 p.m., and the rhythm of the emotional see-saw continued, raising hopes and slamming them to the ground with each start and stop.

At 7:06 p.m., the jury returned with verdicts. The judge reviewed the forms, and there was a brief discussion with the attorneys about how the forms were filled out. All agreed that it was clear what the verdicts were on each of the counts.

The judge instructed Harrell to rise and began to read the verdict.

"'As to Count II, we, the jury, having found the defendant, Harrell Johnson, guilty of Endangering the Welfare of a Child in the First Degree, assess and declare the punishment for Endangering the Welfare of a Child in the First Degree at imprisonment for a term of four years' and the verdict form is signed by the foreperson."

" 'As to Count III, we, the jury, having found the defendant, Harrell L. Johnson, guilty of Abuse of a Child, assess and declare the punishment for Abuse of a Child at imprisonment for a term of 25 years' and again that verdict form is signed by the foreperson."

"The Court accepts the verdicts of the jury in this case, and I will order a sentencing assessment report, and we will schedule a date for sentencing down the road. I should first ask, does either party have any request with regard to the jury before they are discharged?"

Neither side had any more questions. There was nothing left that needed to be said.

The judge discharged the jurors and told the attorneys that they could then talk about setting a date for the hearing on the post-trial motions. He gave them 25 days to get the actions filed and said he set a sentencing date in the future. The court was adjourned. It was 7:17 p.m. and it was over.

The trial had started on October 1, and on October 8, 2008—a mere seven days later—the jury found Harrell Johnson guilty beyond a reasonable doubt. The terror and beatings this little girl endured at the hands of this criminal were unimaginable. She had never known anything but love, so it had to have been horrific for her to try and comprehend what she had done in her short life to deserve this mistreatment. Perhaps with this verdict, Harrell would experience at least a fraction of what he subjected Erica to during the weeks she was his hostage.

Listening to each of the counts being read was an experience of its own. Whether it was the pounding of hearts or the pounding of nails into the box that would enclose Harrell for his lifetime, there was a steady beat as the hammer dropped with each verdict.

Count 1 – Murder, 1st Degree, a Class A Felony

Count 2 – Endanger Welfare of a Child, 1st Degree, a Class D Felony

Count 3 – Child Abuse – Resulting in Death, a Class A Felony

At the end of the trial, detectives and members of the Precious Doe Committee were given copies of the verdict forms that the jury foreperson had signed. The documents were tangible, tactile evidence of a conclusion to a story that hungered for an ending. Finally, something could be filed away, and those who were so close to this case for so many years could start filing the memories of those long years far back in the recesses of their minds and hearts.

Balancing the Scales

October 22, 2008 was justice day for Michelle Green Johnson. She was sentenced to 25 years for her part in her daughter's death. Then, on November 11, 2008, it was Harrell's turn to face his destiny. It took seven years, seven months, and 25 days until the arrival of the sentencing day for Harrell Johnson. Again, he lived up to expectations and took no ownership of his crime. He only claimed to be the actual victim and made excuses—again. Representing the prosecution were Jim Kanatzar, Tim Dollar, and Dawn Parsons. Kenton Hall took the lead on behalf of the defense. The verdict was vindicating, but the sentencing was the declaration of peace to those who had been victimized for far too long.

The usual group of Precious Doe committee members was there, as was the victim advocate assigned to the case, although her position had recently been eliminated. The county didn't think the victims needed a voice, and she fell victim to a budget cut. We were all there to be Erica's voice. It was all over but the shouting, yet no one cried out on her behalf. Oddly enough, the room was very still. The observers were a well-behaved crowd; however, the thought of "off with his head" may very well have been on their minds.

The courthouse was unusually quiet for the circumstances, but that was good. The circus quality that surrounded so much of the case was absent. There were no food vendors, balloons, soothsayers, or body hunters. Instead, the County had ten sheriff's deputies standing before the railing that separated the gallery from the defendant. There was concern that there might be a disturbance in the courtroom, so they took a proactive step with this less-than-subtle show of force. No one misbehaved, however. Harrell wasn't worth the bother of any outbursts from the onlookers. When they brought in Harrell, he was in shackles. He didn't look so tough now.

Harrell's attorneys had submitted a motion to the court for a judgment of acquittal or, in the alternative, for a new trial, but the judge denied this request. It was one last grasp at straws, and it didn't work. So, the lawyers addressed Judge Torrence, and then Harrell was allowed to address the Court.

The following are taken directly from court transcripts: Note that all grammatical and spelling errors are from the original documents, not the author's errors.

MR. KANATZAR: Your Honor, this Court has accepted the jury's verdict in this very important case for this community and the jury has spoken loudly and clearly and I respectfully request that you follow their recommendation as to sentencing. As to murder in the first degree, as you know, there's one penalty that can be imposed, it's like that in the rules, but given the gravity of this case and the way it has affected this community, I also ask that you run the other additional counts consecutively to the murder in the first degree count.

THE COURT: All right. Mr. Hall, do you have any argument you would like to make?

MR. HALL: Your Honor, as the Court knows, the conviction of the murder first-degree charge carries the mandatory sentence of life in prison without parole and the Court has no discretion in that area. As regards to the other two counts, I believe the jury assessed the penalty of four years on the 15 class "D" felony and on the class "A" felony of child abuse resulting in death, I believe the jury imposed a sentence of 25 years after extended deliberations and consideration of the evidence. Judge, we have no additional argument to make in terms of whether the Court should reduce the sentences imposed on Counts II and III from those imposed by the jury. We feel that the controlling sentence is the life without parole sentence, but, Judge, we do feel this case is appropriate and that really justice will be served if the Court imposes concurrent sentences as opposed to consecutive. Primarily, Your Honor, the counts arose out of a single act, a single transaction or a single episode, and consecutive imprisonment on these sentences, we really would have to sort of distort the law and the facts to get there. Admittedly, the community has been put through quite an ordeal with this case from the beginning, 2001 to now, but the ordeal of the community truly is not a factor for the Court to really even consider in determining the central question of should this be consecutive or concurrent. We're certainly understanding and sympathetic of that ordeal and that the entire community feels victimized, but it's important for this Court to maintaining the neutrality of its office and to not be subject to the whims of the community in this respect, especially when it comes to a situation like this which cries out for vengeance and revenge. It's up to this Court to take a measured step back and look at the facts and the law. We feel when the Court does that, that the Court would find that concurrent sentences in this case would serve the ends of justice. Thank you, Your Honor.

THE COURT: Mr. Johnson, it is now time that I ask anybody in a sentencing hearing whether they have anything they'd like to say before I make a decision here and I'll ask that of you. Do you have anything that you would like to say to the Court before I make a decision here?

THE DEFENDANT: Yes, sir, I do, but may I sit up there?

THE COURT: That would be fine. It would be better for us to hear you. Come on up. I tell you what. Why don't--could you remove his leg cuf

THE GUARD: The handcuff stays. It can't be taken off.

THE COURT: All right. Well, do the best you can. Come on up and sit.

(The defendant approached the witness stand.)

THE DEFENDANT: Uh, I just got a few things to say.

THE COURT: You know what, sir? It would help if you would kind of lean closer to the microphone so we hear you better.

THE DEFENDANT: I've just got a few things to say. I'm not going to get off into the legal issues in this case because it really right now don't matter, but I don't want none of you people feeling no sympathy or nothing for me because for one, you people didn't have no sympathy or nothing when my constitutional rights was violated and when I was physically abused and forced to give a statement. I don't want nothing from you people. I was convicted from the start in the eyes of the community and the judicial system and I didn't get a fair trial and I mean I felt that from the start. Don't nobody know, you know, what I'm going through, what I--I got to wake up to this every day. I've got to live with this for the rest of my life. You know, being accused of something like this, you know, someone I loved, you know, you people don't know me. You just know what these people, they cooked up and what I was forced to say. That's all you know. You don't know me, nothing about me. You know, I was there for all of my children and Erica as well. She was my daughter. I made some bad decisions in my life, you know, but never once have I harmed a hair on her head or did anything to hurt her. Like I said, I got to live with what's--this process that I went through. God knows and my little angel knows. Erica knows the truth. And I ain't going to stop fighting until I prove my innocence and the truth is brought to the light. Right now there's no need for me to get off into what my attorneys didn't do or what--the legal issues of this case because it don't matter, and I mean I'm not sitting up here to try to change none of you people's opinions, judgments, because you already had that made from the start and I was. I was a scapegoat for you people to hang this up on. That's all I've got to say.

THE COURT: All right, Mr. Johnson. Thank you.

(The witness returned to the defense table.)

THE COURT: All right. I think it's important to note for the record that the parties and the Court as well, I think, bent over backwards to see that a fair trial in this case was held. I think the weight was strong. The evidence was compelling in support of the jury's verdict. Mr. Johnson, it's apparent that you never have taken and never will take responsibility for your behavior. It's apparent to me that you are a textbook sociopath. You simply don't have the ability to understand, recognize, and feel the pain and the suffering of others.

THE DEFENDANT: You don't know how I feel. All right.

THE COURT: You took the life of an innocent child and, for no reason other than your own selfish desire to avoid being arrested, you watched Erica suffer for hour after hour and die. You waited for nightfall and under the cover of darkness you committed the unspeakable act of cutting off her head with a pair of hedge clippers. For four long years, this community cried for Erica Green. For four long years, this community mourned her. For four long years, this community wondered why nobody came forward and said, "I know who this little girl is. Her name is Erica Green. Everybody wondered how a parent could allow this little girl to remain nameless for so long and then we found out she was Erica Green. A little late. What you did was inhuman and fundamentally incomprehensible. You committed acts that were ghoulish, vile, and by any measure revolting. Erica's nightmare is over. Yours is just beginning.

THE DEFENDANT: Sorry about that.

THE COURT: It will be the judgment and sentence of the Court that the defendant is committed to the custody of the Missouri Division of Adult Institutions for life imprisonment without the possibility of parole on Count I, on Count II for a term of four years in the Missouri Division of Adult Institutions, and on Count III for a term of 25 years in the Missouri Division of Adult Institutions, all of those sentences to run consecutively to each other.

I'm required under our law to make sure, Mr. Johnson, you have full knowledge and understanding of your rights under Supreme Court Rule 24.035. I'm holding here a two-page document that's entitled "Acknowledgment." It's got today's date on it and at the bottom of the second page it appears to have your signature as well. Is that your signature?

THE DEFENDANT: Yep.

THE COURT: All right. Do you have any questions about the information contained in this document?

THE DEFENDANT: No.

MR. HALL: Judge, this case was a special public defender case. I'm submitting a lien for my attorney services. According to the guidelines, it's $6,000 for the case, and that's what I'm submitting. (The Court signed the document.)

THE COURT: Don't spend it all at once.

MR. HALL: It doesn't come close, Judge.

THE COURT: I know.

THE COURT: All right. Anything further to take up here today?

MR. KANATZAR: Not from the state, Your Honor.

MR. HALL: No, Your Honor, not from the defense.

THE COURT: We're adjourned.

What Took You So Long?

In July 2004, Thurman McIntosh attempted to report his information to the police. It was a little over three years after Erica Green's brutal murder. He was challenging to understand, and he couldn't describe her and wasn't sure what her name was. He just knew she was one of Michelle Green's children. A detective followed up on the lead, and Oklahoma Child Welfare said that Michelle's three children by Harrell were in state custody. Erica and another sister were believed to be living with a grandmother in Aurora, Colorado. After some creative police work, it was determined that Michelle Johnson's mother lived in Aurora, Illinois. Child welfare was only off by 969 miles.

Where the breakdown in the Kansas City investigation occurred was that this one detective failed to follow the instructions the squad was given to verify tips. He was supposed to get the child physically identified by someone in Illinois. The Division of Family Services (DFS) records showed that Erica Green and several other children were in Aurora, Illinois. There was an address but what the detective failed to do was to personally contact Aurora, Illinois police and have them go to the address and physically view the children, including the child named Erica Green. Her mother was receiving State welfare for the child. DFS said she was there. The detective questioned the merits of sending someone to track these people down and have someone look at the little girl, given all the information already provided.

From the first days of the investigation, however, Sgt. Bernard insisted it did warrant that level of personal verification, which was the order he gave to the squad. Unfortunately, orders aren't always followed. Corners are sometimes cut. It's called human weakness. We are all flawed and we all make mistakes. This one didn't keep the case from being solved. It just slowed the process down by ten months. The squad had to endure ten more months of stress, defeat, frustration, and accusations. Hebrews 10:36 tells us, "Patient endurance is what you need now, so that you will continue to do God's will. Then you will receive all that he has promised." Endurance was tested repeatedly, and one had to wonder when God would get around to following up on His eternal "to-do" list. It was in His hands and all in His time.

In April 2010, nine years after Erica's murder, her biological father, Larry Green, filed a wrongful death lawsuit in Oklahoma, despite his prior claims that the child did not belong to him. In fairness to Green, even Michelle waivered on the issue of parentage during her May 2005 confession; however, she stated she was about 90% sure her ex-husband had fathered Erica. However, a June 2005 DNA analysis conducted by law enforcement as a part of Erica's murder investigation confirmed that Green was indeed the child's father. Green was incarcerated in Muskogee, Oklahoma, when FBI Special Agent Dirk Tarpley interviewed him shortly after Michelle Johnson's arrest. At that time, he indicated that he and Michelle met in Aurora, Illinois, in the late 1980s and had five children together. He stated his other children lived somewhere in Illinois but was unsure exactly where, as his relationship with them was what he described as nonexistent. Green noted that he and Michelle were not married, although her statements to the police contradicted this. He described them as both being heavy drug users during their time together. He served as her pimp so that she could prostitute herself for drugs or money to support their mutual drug habits. In addition, Green knew that Michelle had a long history of problems with the Illinois and Oklahoma divisions of family services regarding the care of her other four children, with two being born under the influence of cocaine.

Citing her wrongful death and negligence, Larry Green sought compensatory and punitive damages from the Oklahoma Department of Corrections (DOC), Oklahoma University (OU) Medical Center, and the Oklahoma Department of Human Services (DHS) and received an undisclosed settlement. His court-appointed attorney insisted that the purpose was to highlight the lack of communication between the Oklahoma Department of Human Services and the Department of Corrections and the failures to establish policies protecting children born to female inmates while incarcerated. Given Green's lack of interest in his other children sent by his ex-wife back into the home where she experienced abuse, his motives are under suspicion. Green, as documents support, was an adult with a criminal record when he took the minor Michelle Pierce and prostituted her at age 13, violently abused her, and introduced her to drugs in the first place.

Illinois records from 1992 revealed she had failed to protect two of her children from physical abuse involving Larry Green and that she subsequently gave birth to a child by Green, who tested positive for cocaine in 1993. In 1995, the Oklahoma Department of Human Services had been notified that Michelle's fourth child tested positive for cocaine. It was determined that she was still using drugs in 1997 when she was pregnant with Erica. In addition, Green was aware that Michelle's parental rights were terminated for their son, who was born in 1995 and was in the care of Larry's mother before being placed in foster care. Despite this, they had another child, Erica, and records reflect that at least one complaint was lodged with Oklahoma DHS against Michelle, alleging child abuse and neglect involving Erica.

Michelle Johnson was acquainted with Brown through Larry Green's mother, and the hospital and prison officials let Brown take the baby as a temporary foster child. However, there is no written record of what the authorities were told by any of those individuals concerning the personal connections or the transfer of care for the child.

The lawsuit alleged prison officials "performed no background check whatsoever on Ms. Brown" and failed "to adopt or implement any reasonable policies or practices to monitor the care, custody or parental reunification of Erica Green."

The Department of Human Services said it was a Department of Corrections issue that their social services staff should have handled. They claimed it was the mother's responsibility to determine if a family member should take custody of the child. If there were no one to take the child, the hospital would be mandated to report an abandoned baby to DHS, which would then step in and make the child a ward of the state.

At the time of her birth, there were no procedures in place for either DOC or OU Medical Center to provide notification to DHS to connect with the incarcerated mother to assist in planning for the safe placement of the newborn. The lawsuit did bring about a change in procedures so that DHS becomes notified when an inmate gives birth so that a care plan is developed and is in place before the child is released from the hospital, including a background check to determine the fitness of the person taking custody of the infant. However, when Erica was given to Betty Brown, there was only a one-page form to sign, and the only identification shown was her driver's license and a Sam's Club card.

In 2001, the United States Department of Health and Human Services estimated that physical abuse or neglect accounted for over 1,300 child deaths, the majority of which were children under the age of 4 years old. The system designed to protect our most precious commodity failed countless children; it was an unspeakable tragedy.

The discarded child, once known only as "Precious Doe", proved to be a profit center for both Thurman McIntosh and Larry Green long after her death despite their apathy toward the living child. In a podcast interview years later, Michelle Johnson expressed her anger regarding the lawsuit and Green's failure to share the settlement. She stated that Green gave $3,000 to their oldest child but did not give any money to Erica's other siblings. She indicated that she went to prison for stealing to get money to buy him drugs; however, she did note that he sent her $300. Fraudulent welfare payments, rewards, lawsuits—the money seemed to flow, yet it was up to concerned strangers to solicit donations to simply give the unknown little waif a decent burial.

Prostitution may be considered the oldest profession, but murder holds the distinction of being the first violent crime. Cain and Abel set in motion behaviors that have withstood the test of time. The great religious texts don't tell us how Abel died, just that Cain killed him. We know it wasn't with a gun or a knife. Cain was a farmer and may have used a rock, a primitive tool, or maybe he was like Harrell Johnson and kicked his victim to death. They both were angry, jealous, covetous, and brutal. Neither could restrain his impulse to destroy something precious. No one anywhere, at any time, despite the cries for gun control or more police presence, will ever prevent violent crime. Not as long as humans like Harrell walk the face of the Earth, for among us tread the children of Cain.

Epilogue

It is a widely known fact that our family has assumed an "Addams Family-like" persona over the last 20 years. In 1994, David had been in Homicide for four years. Four years of too much overtime, not enough leads, and day-to-day confrontation of horrors unimaginable to anyone other than Stephen King on a particularly lucrative day. Dinnertime conversations often had to be regulated as too gross or too darkly humorous for a "kids in the room" audience. Sometimes our adult friends—-a little over-zealous from exposure to TV crime dramas—got a little queasy when they'd probed for gory crime scene descriptions and received the detailed accounts they'd requested but couldn't handle. Who could?

With two children at home, I was left to deal with a full-time job as a hospital administrator, night classes to finish for a master's degree, Cub Scouts, Little League, high school plays, and everything else that needed addressing. David's focus was tunneled, intense, and elusive to his family. His cases took up all his waking hours, and his victims walked with him in his sleep, haunting what should have been a respite from this horror. It would be years before I could accept taking a back seat role to his investigations. I wondered then—and still do—if I ever made it as a subconscious "ride along" guest in his unmarked car. I could comprehend the demands—I'd been a police sergeant in the reserves for ten years. It's simple to analyze the psychological impact that this specialized line of work demands of its detectives. My objectivity, however, stopped at the door to my own house. I'd plead with David to please leave the cases at headquarters; please leave the cases in the car; please leave the cases outside our house, in the garage, maybe? No luck. They came home with him, the victims clinging to his clothes. His sport coat was weighted down with a pager, two cell phones, handcuffs, badge case, notepad, pen, and the burden of lost children heavy on his shoulders. Then, in 1994, one ghostly little spirit came to our home, grasping his pant leg, hiding in the back of his mind. She silently overtook our home and our hearts. She lurked around the house and took a seat at our table, where she remained for eight long years. When she gave up her chair in exchange for a permanent resting place, another little girl came and sat down in her spot. "Precious Doe" would remain there for another three years.

Those years would prove to be particularly difficult for our family as the tremendous pressure of Erica's case, coupled with all the new homicides to investigate, bore down on David. It took a heavy toll, but we managed to wade through the muck and mire we were entrenched in, paying a penance of sorts for someone else's sins. Psalm 40:2 states it most succinctly: *"I waited patiently for the LORD; he turned to me and heard my cry. He lifted me out of the slimy pit, out of the mud and mire; he set my feet on a rock and gave me a firm place to stand. He put a new song in my mouth, a hymn of praise to our God. Many will see and fear and put their trust in the LORD."*

On the day of Harrell's sentencing, David and I sat in the first row of the gallery, and I recall looking around and seeing the faces of so many others who, each for their own reason, were invested in seeing justice for Erica Green brought to fruition. We were all waiting, rather impatiently, for silent prayers to be answered. It was a "Madame

Defarge" moment. Sitting there, I was writing some notes instead of crocheting, but it had a front-row-seat-at-the-guillotine quality about it all the same. Mine, however, was not the blood-thirsting quest for retribution that Thérèse Defarge sought in Charles Dickens's *A Tale of Two Cities*. Instead, it was closure that I desired. Closure and peace. For my husband, my family, and a community whose collective heart ached for this discarded little girl who now had a name. The Dalai Lama said that you should judge your success by what you had to give up to get it. This was a successful outcome to a long ordeal, but the sacrifices made seemed too great a price to pay for such a hollow victory.

After the verdict was read and the judge had dispensed with the final, miscellaneous details—the boring bits of paperwork accompanying the recording of the final outcome of a long-awaited sentence, the court was dismissed. It was 10:40 a.m. and it was time to let the healing begin in earnest. After the sentencing, we crowded onto an already-occupied courthouse elevator, and no one spoke until we stopped on the first floor. There was so much to say, and yet the silence spoke volumes. Finally, it was all over, but the shoutin', and yet no one seemed to find the words. Finally, when everyone began to exit, we heard a woman say they had meant to get off on the second floor.

We were all reasonably dazed when we were herded onto the elevator, and I guess no one had noticed them, so they didn't get to squeeze off the packed elevator when it had stopped on the prior floor. I turned around and looked down. A little girl who looked like Erica was standing there. I held my breath for a moment, glancing over at David. He looked like he saw a ghost. I bent down and spoke to the little girl.

"Hi, baby. How old are you?"

Her mother answered for her. "Three years old."

Weird isn't it? Maybe the heavens were trying to send us a message that Erica was okay, that this part of the journey was over, and life would go on.

On April 25, 2009, a march was held by the Precious Doe Committee to raise money to try and purchase the 5 acres of vacant land that was part of the area where Erica's body was dumped. The fundraising was headed up by Tim Dollar, the prosecutor who got Harrell's conviction. Through the efforts of his amazing assistant, Stefani Brancato, who coordinated it, over 200 people participated in the walk for Erica Green. Participants walked from 63rd and Elmwood to 59th and Kensington, where Jackson County had erected a portable stage. There were numerous speakers but not much of a presence from the media. It garnered a little coverage, but it wasn't considered newsworthy by now. Even the funnel cake guy wasn't interested. It was sad because the area could be a safe place for children. Cleaning up that makeshift dump/graveyard would have benefited the residents of 64130—the deadliest zip code in the Kansas City metropolitan area. Unfortunately, Dollar's dream of improving a neighborhood so desperate for change never came to fruition.

Detective Danny Phillips and his wife attended the march, and while we waited for the program to begin, we walked down the pathway to where Erica was found. Seeing David and Danny retracing those steps was a powerful and emotional scene. They were stoic, but their eyes told the whole story. Those indeed are the windows to the soul, for you could see the unwavering commitment to this little girl—the pressure, the emotion bubbling up from the depths of those souls. There was still trash strewn about, and a make-shift memorial was there, but the city trucks that used that path had crushed the flowers, the signs, and what appeared to be a small plastic cast statue. It wasn't easy to make out what it was. All that was left were shards, except for a wing. It was embedded in the mud, but it was still intact. I couldn't tell if it was supposed to be that of an angel or a bird, but I pulled it out, brushed it off, and slipped it into my pocket.

The little broken wing now sits on a bookcase in my office. It lies next to a copy of my favorite book, *To Kill a Mockingbird,* and a statue of a small mourning dove that looks like she's guarding it. The room has a collection of vintage books by Charles Dickens and Victor Hugo and artwork depicting great authors and etchings of orphans. There's a large garden angel that Christine Stevens hand-painted and gave to us in memory of Angel Hart. The room inspires penning the macabre as well as the motivational. It goes back to my way of looking at a sadder side of life, fending off my own demons, and adopting what needs a home. It has the tired, the poor, the huddled masses, and the broken bits of the dearly departed. So the misfit little angel's wing from the "Precious Doe" crime scene seems to fit right in.

Every Memorial Day, we make the rounds to several local cemeteries or grave gardens, as our grandson calls them, taking flowers to loved ones and friends who have passed on. It has become a ritual of sorts to meet my brother for lunch and then we head down the road to the cemetery where my father, Angel Hart, and a family friend who was like a second father to David, are all buried. From there, we go to St. Mary's to place flowers for my relatives and Amanda's best friend from high school. The last stop is Memorial Park, where David's parents and grandparents are buried. My mother and a great-aunt are also buried there, and we have our own plots purchased near them. Finally, straight up the road, high atop a hill, Erica Michelle Marie

Green rests. Six degrees of separation and a six-hundred-foot distance between our eternal connections.

The ancient pagans said: "The mills of the gods grind slowly, but they grind exceedingly fine." It's thought that this expression was the origin of the phrase "the wheels of justice turn exceedingly slow." In David's line of work as a homicide detective, one feels that if justice has wheels, the tires must be flat or at least really low. At best, it's a bumpy ride on the justice bus, and getting to where you need to go is hard. However, sometimes the hard work pays off, and a case comes together. They solve it quickly and can feel like they made it to the final destination—an arrest and conviction. But in this line of work, murder is tragic and, unfortunately, all too common, so it's back on the bus.

While the wheels of justice crank slowly, the wheels in the mind of a dedicated detective whirl non-stop. Old cases he's worked on often spin through David's head, and he's attuned to details he can recite on demand. A bit of information he hears in an interview—a name, a car description, an address—can trigger a memory about another case and send him down a path that might actually bring a new and solid lead to what had been a cold case. At the most unexpected moments, a sight or a sound can derail a conversation from "I took the car in to be looked at, and the mechanic said…" into "That's the road where Crystal Kipper's car broke down." I continually remind David that we can't drive down I-29 without his instantly shifting mental gears and mentioning the case of a young girl believed to have been murdered, but her body was never found. I know he honestly is not aware that he does it. It's what I call his "O.D.D." - Obsessive Detective Disease or "odd," if you will. This is how the victims deeply affect these men and women and stay awake or asleep with them. David can't match a tie and a suit jacket because it's not essential to him, but he can hear an address and precisely tell you all the case details. Because it's central to what he does—the hub in that mental wheel because it's not a file number—it's a human being.

From a detective's point of view, the criminal justice system seems just that—justice for the criminals, not the victims. In every case, they have to measure each step they take and each decision they make to see how it fits in the legal system. A reasonable defense attorney has months to pick apart a decision they had to make in minutes to protect a crime scene or find a witness. A killer can make 100 mistakes—detectives can't make any. One misstep and the case will get thrown out on a technicality, and the wheels of justice suddenly fall off.

Often, the victim's families think detectives aren't telling them everything they know. There are times when information has to be kept close to the vest. Holding some details back is necessary to protect some critical facts. It becomes information that only the detective and the killer know. What's the hardest for a detective is when a family won't cooperate and tell everything they know. Suspects get protected, and witnesses go silent. And the detectives feel that they're the only ones that care about the victim. Their respective mothers' boyfriends murdered five-year-old Angel Hart and four-year-old Erica Green. Hearing their mothers utter the words, "but I love him," are crimes in and of themselves. It's like peeling an onion. It stinks, and it makes your eyes water. But as the layers are peeled back, it generally reveals that the mothers were once abuse victims themselves in one form or another. Cases like these happen all too often. The cycle continues, and it's one of those spinning wheels that roll along on the justice bus. If momma won't give him up, the tire goes flat. It's up to the detectives to find another avenue to pump it up.

As detectives, they take these cases to heart and become a part of their lives and the lives of their family members. Angel Hart was learning her alphabet. Erica Green's favorite song was "The Wheels on the Bus." Our grandson was born on Crystal Kipper's birthday. The details stay with the detectives as permanent imprints on their hearts. Dave does his job because he still believes in what he does. He's still convinced that even though the justice wheels turn slowly, sooner or later, justice is served.

And, like the circle of life, the wheels on the bus go 'round and 'round.

Acknowledgments

Death brings with it strange connections. You end up with an extended family united by loss. We are guests at events held by Parents of Murdered Children. We have so many dear friends that we have come to know through the ugliest and darkest times in this strange world of violence and untimely death. They are beacons of hope in our lives. I guess that's how you find each other. During your darkest hours, you follow the light.

It would be futile to try and acknowledge all the individuals who helped in some way to bring these angels home. I have mentioned many key people in the book and sincerely apologize for oversights. How do you list every name of everyone in greater Kansas City and beyond? These stories took on national and international notoriety and, as such, touched an infinite number of lives. Suffice it to say it is with humility, endless gratitude, and boundless love that I thank you for being a part of this story.

The Detectives of the 1020 Squad:

James Agnew, Jeffrey Cowdrey, Eric Dillenkoffer, Michael Hutcheson, Wayne Jones, Keith Kirchhoff, Steven Miller, Tammy Payne, Danny Phillips, Chris Price, Robert Rickett, Roy Rogers, Derek Rothert, Bruce Solomon, Teddy Taylor, John Thompson.

Sincerest thanks to Josephine Meyers and Christine Stevens for never letting me give up on this story; to my family and friends for their unwavering support; to the late Mary Roll for believing in my writing; to Betty Brown for sharing her photos of her precious Erica with me, and to the friendship extended to us by the members of the Precious Doe Committee:

Marcie Williams, LaDonna Deboe, Yvonne Deboe, Annette Johnson, Cynthia Cannady, Christine Dunn, Calvin Neal, George Tyler, Jermaine Reed, and Melissa Robinson.

For More News About Marla Bernard,
Signup For Our Newsletter:

http://wbp.bz/newsletter

Word-of-mouth is critical to an author's long-term success. If you appreciated this book please leave a review on the Amazon sales page:

http://wbp.bz/precious

AVAILABLE FROM JOHN WESLEY ANDERSON AND WILDBLUE PRESS

A Legendary Lawman's Quest To Solve A Child Beauty Queen's Murder

John Wesley Anderson

http://wbp.bz/louandjonbenet

AVAILABLE FROM STEVE JACKSON AND WILDBLUE PRESS

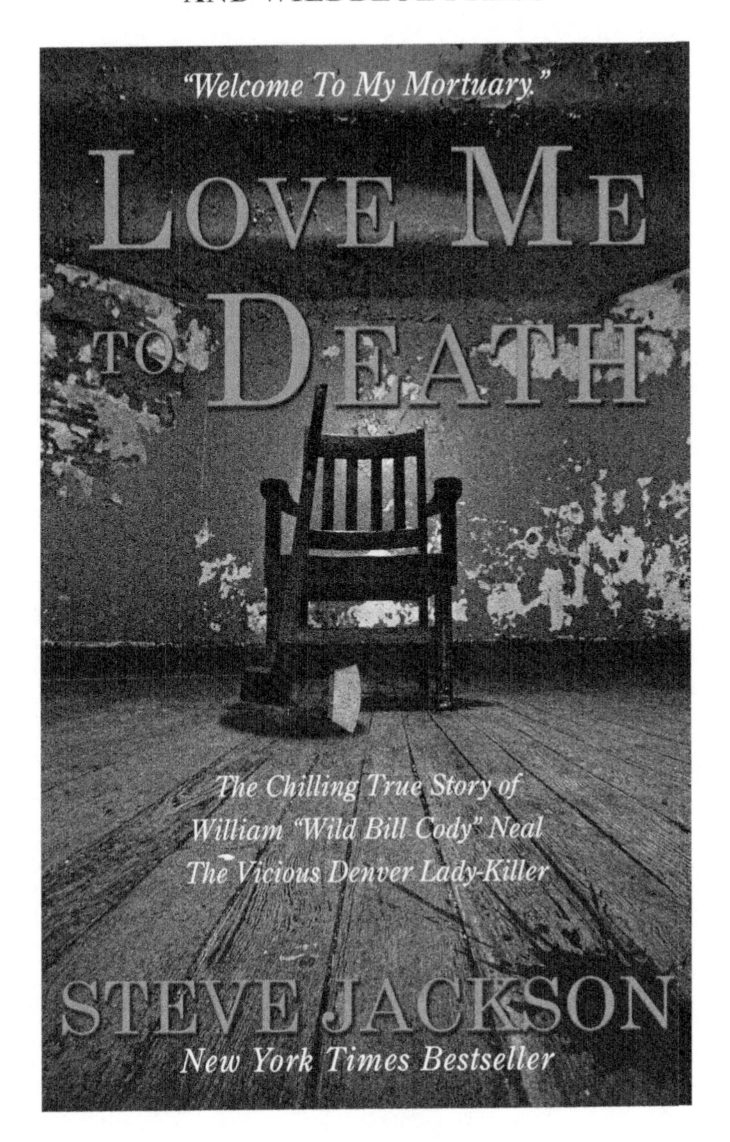

http://wbp.bz/loveme